HELL FIGHTS WHAT IT FEARS

Copyright © 2025 by Dr. Brenda Jefferson

All Scripture quotations, unless otherwise noted, taken from THE HOLY BIBLE, NEW INTERNATIONAL VERSION®, NIV® Copyright © 1973, 1978, 1984, 2011 by Biblica, Inc.® Used by permission. All rights reserved worldwide.

Scripture quotations marked KJV taken from The Holy Bible, King James Version. Cambridge Edition: 1769. Scripture quotations marked AMP are taken from the Amplified® Bible (AMP), Copyright © 2015 by The Lockman Foundation. Used by permission. www.Lockman.org. Scripture quotations marked NKJV are taken from the New King James Version®. Copyright © 1982 by Thomas Nelson. Used by permission. All rights reserved.

All rights reserved, including the right to reproduce this book or portions thereof in any form whatsoever. For information, address info@drbrendaj.org or visit www.drbrendaj.org for more information.

Library of Congress Cataloging-in-Publication Data is available.

ISBN 978-1-7365-4659-8
ISBN 978-1-7365-4659-8 (eBook)

This book is dedicated to everyone who has ever felt the weight of the enemy's attack — to every person who has wrestled with discouragement, who has battled fear, who has been told they are too broken, too late, or too unworthy.

To you who have been pressed on every side — know this: the enemy wants to steal, kill, and destroy (John 10:10), but God has declared life, identity, purpose, and victory over you. This book is for the fighters, the wounded, the weary, the ones who feel unseen or forgotten — and it is written as a reminder that hell fights what it fears, and what it fears most is the destiny and power you carry in Christ.

With deepest love, I also dedicate this book to my beloved husband, Bishop M.B. Jefferson, who has stood beside me faithfully for nearly 50 years of preaching the unadulterated Word of God. His unwavering support has been the steady foundation that has allowed me to minister, write, and carry out the call God placed on my life. Without his covering and partnership, I could not have walked this journey.

To every soul holding onto hope — this book is for you.

With all my heart,

Dr. Brenda Jefferson

How to Use This Book

Read With Expectation

Each chapter in *Hell Fights What It Fears* is designed as a strategic round of spiritual training—short enough to read in one sitting, strong enough to shift your perspective.

1. **Opening Question & Intro** – Pause and let the question linger. It primes your heart for the theme and invites the Holy Spirit to spotlight what you personally need today.

2. **Affirmations** – Speak them **out loud**. Hearing truth in your own voice rewires fear-based thinking and releases faith into the atmosphere.

3. **Pull-Out Quote** – Treat this like a rally cry. Write it on a sticky note, post it on your mirror, or share it on social media to encourage others.

Feel free to underline, highlight, or journal in the margins. Your copy of this book is meant to look *used*, not pristine—scuffed pages are evidence of practiced victory.

Engage the 5-Minute Victory Journal

Immediately after each chapter you'll find a guided page. It turns revelation into transformation in just five focused minutes.

Step	What You Do	Why It Matters
1. Key Verse Focus	Read the verse, circle the word that strikes you, write one sentence on why.	Anchors your mind to Scripture as the final authority.
2. Gratitude Glance	List one thing you're thankful for today.	Gratitude shifts your heart from survival mode to faith mode.
3. Today's Battle & Truth	Name the loudest pressure, then answer it with a truth from the chapter.	Identifies the real fight and arms you with a specific promise.
4. Speak It ✚ Sign It	Read the declaration aloud, fill in the blank, initial beside it.	Puts prophetic words in your mouth and seals them with commitment.
5. Next Step + Amen	Write one practical action for the next 24 hours, finish the one-line prayer.	Converts inspiration into obedience and invites God to empower it.

Time investment: ≈ 1 minute per step, 5 minutes total.

Materials needed: A pen, an honest heart, and a willing spirit.

Tips for Maximum Impact

- **Morning Momentum:** Tackle the journal first thing in the day; it frames your mindset before the world does.

- **Evening Reflection:** Reread your declaration before bed. Let it echo in your thoughts as you sleep.

- **Accountability Partner:** Share one takeaway and your "next step" with a friend each week. Victory grows in community.

- **Reuse in New Battles:** When fresh opposition hits, flip back to the chapter whose truth addresses it and redo the journal page. The Word never expires.

Final Encouragement

This book is not a souvenir; it's a sword. The journal is not busywork; it's weapons training. Lean in. Write boldly. Speak loudly. Live fearlessly. Heaven has marked you, hell fears you, and these pages will help you walk in that reality—five minutes at a time.

CONTENTS

01 pg. 1
YOU ARE NOT UNDER ATTACK BECAUSE YOU ARE WEAK

02 pg. 10
EVIDENCE THAT YOU ARE MARKED

03 pg. 20
HAVE YOU BEEN INQUIRED ABOUT?

04 pg. 30
THE WEAPON HELL COULDN'T KILL

05 pg. 39
WHEN DESTINY GETS INTERRUPTED

06 pg. 49
WHEN HELL RINGS ALARMS

07 pg. 59
WHEN HELL INVESTIGATES YOUR POTENTIAL

08 pg. 68
THE BREAKING THAT BUILT YOU

09 pg. 77
THE PURPOSE BEHIND THE PRESSURE

10 pg. 86
THE WEAPON HELL COULDN'T KILL — YOU

11 pg. 95
FAITH IN THE FIRE

12 pg. 103
THE ALARM OF YOUR ASSIGNMENT

13 pg. 112
VICTORY IN THE VALLEY

14 pg. 122
WHEN GOD SAYS LIVE

15 pg. 132
DECLARATIONS AND THE AFTERMATH OF WAR

16 pg. 143
HOW TO USE SCRIPTURE BULLETS

17 pg. 152
THE PROOF THAT HELL FAILED

18 pg. 161
PRAYER AND DECLARATION OF IDENTITY

19 pg. 169
A DECLARATION OF ENDURANCE

20 pg. 177
CHARGE: HEAVEN'S WEAPON, HELL'S THREAT

21 pg. 185
MY PERSONAL TESTIMONY

YOU ARE NOT UNDER ATTACK BECAUSE YOU ARE WEAK

BRENDAJEFFERSON.COM

01
CHAPTER ONE

Have you ever stopped to ask why spiritual warfare seems to find you even before you find the spotlight?

From the moment Heaven marked your life, alarms sounded in the unseen realm. The attacks you face are not proof of weakness, but proof that you carry weight an assignment hell cannot afford to ignore. This chapter reframes resistance as Heaven's vote of confidence that you are equipped to disrupt darkness.

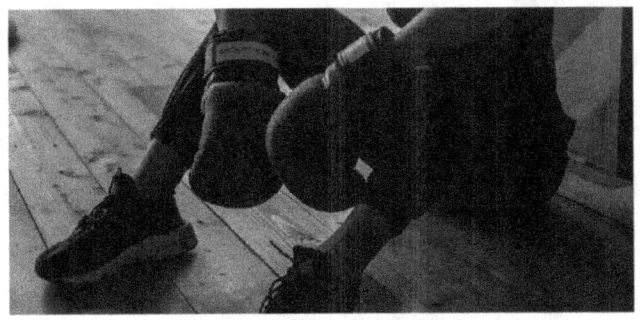

You're Not Under Attack Because You're Weak

You're not under attack because you're weak; you're under attack because you're a threat. Hell doesn't waste its weapons on those going nowhere; it targets those carrying Heaven's assignments—those whom Hell fears will shake the ground and set captives free. You are dangerous to the kingdom of darkness. You are a living threat to the plans of the enemy. You are walking proof that light still breaks through, that prayers still shift atmospheres, that obedience still dismantles strongholds.

You weren't born into a neutral space. You were born onto a battlefield.

The moment your life entered the earth, alarms sounded in the unseen realm. Not because of who you were then — but because of who you were becoming. Hell took notice, not when you stood on a stage or when people began to know your name. Hell marked you before your first breakthrough, your first sermon, your first prayer.

Why? Because you were carrying something hell couldn't kill, silence, or steal.

Marked Before You Were Ready

You didn't have to do anything wrong to draw warfare. In fact, some of the greatest warfare came before you even knew how to fight. That's the evidence you were marked early. Joseph didn't provoke his brothers by pride — his dream did. David wasn't hated by Saul because of ambition — it was the anointing oil still soaking in his hair.

Some of the early pain in your life wasn't random — it was spiritual interference. Hell tries to abort what heaven appoints. And the attack wasn't confirmation of your failure — it was confirmation of your weight.

You carried something, even when you didn't know what it was. You carried glory. You carried a word. You carried deliverance in your spirit for people you hadn't even met. And every time you chose not to quit — you confirmed what hell feared the most: You're dangerous to darkness.

The Misunderstanding of Warfare

Many people mistake warfare as a sign of weakness or failure. But what if it's the opposite? What if warfare is the announcement of heaven's trust?

If God allowed it, it wasn't abandonment — it was investment. God trusted you with resistance because He already placed resilience inside of you.

Satan doesn't waste resources. He assigns opposition where there is potential. If you've ever wondered why some seasons hit you harder than others, it's because your next season was heavier with glory than the last.

Why Hell Reacts to You

Hell doesn't react to noise. It reacts to sound.

Your sound — your intercession, your worship, your obedience — shakes the foundations of darkness. Hell doesn't flinch when we complain. But it trembles when we obey. That's why the greatest attacks usually come after you say "yes" to God.

Obedience triggers demonic agitation. But it also summons angelic reinforcement.

What you carry — your mantle, your mission, your prophetic voice — it registers in hell's database as a threat level. It's not personal. It's spiritual. And that's what makes you unstoppable.

When You Don't Know Why You're Being Fought

There will be seasons when you won't even know what's happening. You'll look around and say, "Why now? Why me?" But those are often the times heaven is increasing your rank.

You don't need a microphone to be dangerous. Some of the most powerful threats to hell are people who pray in silence, war in worship, and walk in purity. Their name isn't famous on earth — but it's known in heaven and hell.

"Jesus I know, and Paul I know; but who are ye?" — Acts 19:15 KJV

That means hell keeps files. It knows names. And it recognizes divine authority when it sees it.

CHAPTER ONE
FAITH-BUILDING AFFIRMATIONS

01

I am a recognized threat to the kingdom of darkness, not a helpless target

02

My present battles confirm Heaven's trust in the resilience God has already placed within me

03

Every act of obedience I offer summons angelic reinforcement and dismantles strongholds around me

Reflection: Why Has Hell Been After You?

Take a moment.

Think about every fight, every failure, every season you barely made it through. Now ask yourself: Was it all coincidence? Or was there something in me the enemy couldn't afford to see released?

You don't just carry potential. You carry prophecy.

And prophecy scares hell.

The resistance was never about what you lost — it was about what you were destined to release. Your life is proof that the enemy's plans failed. You are still here. You are still standing. And you're rising with fire in your bones.

So when you feel resistance, don't panic. Smile. Because it means you've been recognized in hell — and feared.

If you've ever wondered why your life has felt like a war zone, this is why. The attacks weren't random. The betrayals weren't accidents. The resistance wasn't punishment; it was evidence.

> " You're not under attack because you're weak; you're under attack because you're a threat."

THOUGHTS:

_____
_____
_____
_____
_____
_____

5 MINUTE VICTORY JOURNAL

TAKE A MOMENT TO REFLECT

DATE

S M T W T F S

CHAPTER 1
"YOU'RE NOT UNDER ATTACK BECAUSE YOU'RE WEAK"

KEY VERSE FOCUS:

PRESSURE I FEEL:

IN THE NEXT 24 HOURS I WILL:

> "And the evil spirit answered and said, Jesus I know, and Paul I know; but who are ye?"
>
> —Acts 19:15

Father I Thank you for:

☺
☺
☺

I AM A RECOGNIZED THREAT TO DARKNESS BECAUSE:

TRUTH FROM THIS CHAPTER:

NOTES & FREE THOUGHTS:

CHAPTER TWO

EVIDENCE THAT YOU ARE MARKED

BRENDAJEFFERSON.COM

02
CHAPTER TWO

When sudden pressure surrounds you, do you view it as a random storm—or as courtroom evidence that heaven has already stamped you with significance?

Hell never wastes ammunition. The very resistance closing in on you is proof that you are "pregnant with breakthrough," carrying an anointing powerful enough to break generational cycles and birth something heaven-breathed and hell-feared

Evidence That You Are Marked

Evidence That You Are Marked, Evidence That You Are Anointed, Evidence that you are carrying something Hell cannot afford to see born. What you are carrying is bigger than you. It's a threat to systems, to cycles, to every generational curse that thought it could live forever in your bloodline. This is not the time to bow. This is the time to build. This is not the time to break. This is the time to birth. This book is a war manual for those Hell thought it could stop. It's a survival guide for those the enemy couldn't silence. It's for the ones who refuse to die with their destiny buried inside them. Because Hell fights what it fears—and it fears you.

Evidence That You Are Marked. Evidence That You Are Anointed. Evidence That You Are Carrying Something Hell Cannot Afford to See Born.

This isn't a poetic phrase. It's a spiritual reality. Hell doesn't fight what doesn't matter. Hell doesn't study the ordinary. It doesn't waste resources on people who pose no threat. You were fought because you carry something heaven-breathed — and hell-feared.

What's inside of you isn't just purpose — it's warfare. It's deliverance. It's disruption to the patterns of hell. You are carrying answers to ancient prayers. You are the next move of God in someone's bloodline. You are the shift hell thought it could delay.

You Are Pregnant With Breakthrough

This is not about emotion. This is about evidence. You are pregnant with something spiritual — something eternal — and the contractions of warfare are proof that delivery is near.

You've been attacked not because of weakness, but because of womb — a spiritual womb housing revival, healing, and legacy. And hell knows if you ever fully walk in it... whole regions will shift.

That's why the enemy came for your voice. That's why he came for your mind. That's why he targeted your family. Because you carry something generational.

"Before I formed thee in the belly I knew thee; and before thou camest forth out of the womb I sanctified thee, and I ordained thee..." (Jeremiah 1:5, KJV)

You were chosen before you were conscious. Marked before you were mature. Targeted before you were trained.

The Real Reason You've Been Fought

This is not the time to bow. This is the time to build. This is not the time to break. This is the time to birth.

Hell knows that if you birth what's inside of you, the ripple effect will be unstoppable. The strongholds you're breaking now will not be rebuilt. The cycles you're ending now will not be inherited. The fire you're walking in now will spread to others — and hell fears that spread.

You've been fought because you were chosen to end what others tolerated, and to start what others only dreamed of.

This is not just about survival. This is about legacy.

The Greater the Threat, the Greater the Target

The oil on your life draws attention in the spirit realm. When David was anointed, immediately Saul began to hate him. When Jesus was baptized, immediately He was driven into the wilderness to be tempted.

Why? Because spiritual recognition brings spiritual resistance.

"Think it not strange concerning the fiery trial which is to try you..." (1 Peter 4:12, KJV)

Hell doesn't fight the unmarked. It fights the rising ones, the burning ones, the obedient ones.

You are being fought because you are feared.

This Is Your Building Season

You are carrying something that disrupts:

- Systems of oppression
- Cycles of dysfunction
- Generational curses that thought they could reign in your family forever

This is why the enemy sent opposition. This is why the timing of the attacks has been so calculated.

But hear this: God did not send you into this world to be defeated. He sent you as a builder, a birther, a breaker of chains.

And this chapter — your life right now — is the evidence that you are too dangerous to be left alone.

CHAPTER TWO
FAITH-BUILDING AFFIRMATIONS

01

I am unmistakably marked by God, and hell's hostility is simply proof of that mark

02

I am pregnant with divine breakthrough; every contraction of warfare signals that delivery is near

03

This is my building season—I rise to construct what heaven ordained and destroy what hell once controlled

Reflection: Evidence, Not Coincidence

Let this settle in your spirit:

- That betrayal? Evidence.
- That heaviness? Evidence.
- That battle that came out of nowhere? Evidence.
- That fire you're walking through? Evidence.

Evidence that you are marked. Evidence that you are anointed. Evidence that you are carrying something hell cannot afford to see born.

So don't stop. Don't fold. Don't shrink.

This is not the time to second-guess what's in you. It's time to go full-term and deliver the destiny you've been carrying all along.

Because hell fights what it fears — and it fears you.

> **You were fought because you carry something heaven-breathed and hell-feared**

THOUGHTS:

_____
_____
_____
_____
_____
_____

5 MINUTE VICTORY JOURNAL

CHAPTER 2
"EVIDENCE THAT YOU ARE MARKED"

TAKE A MOMENT TO REFLECT

DATE

S M T W T F S

KEY VERSE FOCUS:

"From henceforth let no man trouble me: for I bear in my body the marks of the Lord Jesus."

—Galatians 6:17

PRESSURE I FEEL:

IN THE NEXT 24 HOURS I WILL:

Father I thank you for:

- ☺
- ☺
- ☺

I AM A RECOGNIZED THREAT TO DARKNESS BECAUSE:

TRUTH FROM THIS CHAPTER:

NOTES & FREE THOUGHTS:

CHAPTER THREE

HAVE YOU BEEN INQUIRED ABOUT?

BRENDAJEFFERSON.COM

03
CHAPTER THREE

When pressure shows up like an audit on every area of your life, do you see it as punishment—or as proof that hell has filed a formal inquiry because heaven already trusts you?

Spiritual opposition is rarely random. The very fact that darkness is taking notes on your movements is evidence that you carry an assignment worth tracking, just as Job and Peter did when Satan "desired to have" them.

Have You Been Inquired About?

You want to know if you're a threat? Look at the size of your battle. Hell doesn't fight what it can control. Hell doesn't fight what is already asleep. Hell doesn't fight what is comfortable playing small. Hell fights what it fears will wake up, rise up, and tear up the enemy's camp.

Some of you are wondering why you were attacked before you could fully step into your calling. Before the business started. Before the ministry grew. Before the promise was fulfilled. It's because the enemy saw it before you did. The inquiry in hell's camp wasn't about who you were today; it was about who you were becoming. The enemy isn't fighting you over your past; he's fighting you over your future.

Every destiny has an origin — but not every origin is obvious.

There are some who go through life misunderstood, attacked, delayed, and resisted, and they wonder why hell seems so invested in their destruction. But the truth is: hell has inquired about you.

Just as Satan inquired about Job, there is a spiritual investigation happening behind the scenes. Hell doesn't attack without cause — it attacks because of what you carry.

Hell's Surveillance

In Job 1:7–8 (KJV), the Bible reads: "And the Lord said unto Satan, Whence comest thou? Then Satan answered the Lord, and said, From going to and fro in the earth, and from walking up and down in it. And the Lord said unto Satan, Hast thou considered my servant Job...?"

This was not just casual conversation. This was an unveiling of spiritual surveillance. Satan had been watching Job. He had noticed the hedge around him, the favor, the fruit, the fear of God. And hell was taking notes.

You must understand: hell keeps records. It studies patterns. It watches how you respond to pressure. It monitors your spiritual growth. The moment you become a threat, the whispers in the realm of darkness turn into targeted warfare.

Heaven's Confidence vs. Hell's Curiosity

God didn't hesitate to call Job "My servant." Heaven had confidence in Job's integrity. But that very confidence stirred hell's curiosity. Hell always asks: "What will they do if I strike their health? Their finances? Their family?"

This is not just about suffering. It's about proving that your faith is not for sale. That your worship isn't tied to circumstances. That your yes remains even when your world shakes.

Job's story wasn't just about loss — it was about the power of loyalty under fire.

Why the Enemy Requests Access

Satan does not have unlimited access. He must ask. He must inquire. This should encourage you: nothing touches you unless God allows it — and if God allows it, there's purpose in it.

Luke 22:31–32 (KJV) gives us another example: "And the Lord said, Simon, Simon, behold, Satan hath desired to have you, that he may sift you as wheat: But I have prayed for thee, that thy faith fail not…"

Even Peter — flawed, impulsive, still learning — was the subject of satanic interest. Why? Because Jesus already saw Peter's future. A future preacher. A pillar of the early church. A man whose voice would shake regions. Hell inquired because heaven had invested.

When You're Targeted Because You're Trusted

The inquiry of hell is not a death sentence — it's a signpost. It says: "You matter in this war."

You were never insignificant. You were always carrying something that, if unleashed, would bring damage to darkness. That's why hell asked for access — but God placed boundaries.

Even in suffering, God's sovereignty rules. The enemy may touch circumstances, but he can't touch the seal on your soul.

The Power of Endurance

When Job lost everything, he worshipped.

That one act broke the rules of hell's expectation. Hell assumed that if Job lost his blessings, he'd curse God. But Job did what confounded darkness:

He bowed. He blessed. He endured.

Hell can't calculate the strength of a made-up mind.

So when you're in a season of intense pressure, don't always ask, "Why me?" Sometimes the better question is, "What is heaven trying to reveal through me?"

CHAPTER THREE
FAITH-BUILDING AFFIRMATIONS

01

I am on heaven's honor roll, and hell's surveillance only confirms my worth in God's eyes.

02

Every request the enemy makes must pass through God's permission, so my battles come with built-in purpose.

03

I am trusted to endure; what tries to sift me today will only reveal unshakeable faith tomorrow.

Reflection: Have You Been Inquired About?

Take time to reflect on the resistance you've faced. What if your trials are not a sign of abandonment but a sign of divine trust?

What if the enemy's request for access was because he feared what you would become if you ever healed, if you ever stepped into wholeness, if you ever walked fully in your calling?

You are not under attack because you're weak — but because you're a weapon.

And hell is afraid of what happens when you wake up and realize that the fight wasn't to destroy you — it was to announce you.

> **You were fought because you carry something heaven-breathed and hell-feared**

THOUGHTS:

_____
_____
_____
_____
_____
_____

5 MINUTE VICTORY JOURNAL

TAKE A MOMENT TO REFLECT

DATE

S   M   T   W   T   F   S

CHAPTER 3
"HAVE YOU BEEN INQUIRED ABOUT?"

KEY VERSE FOCUS:

"And the Lord said, Simon, Simon, behold, Satan hath desired to have you, that he may sift you as wheat: But I have prayed for thee, that thy faith fail not."

—Luke 22:31-32

PRESSURE I FEEL:

IN THE NEXT 24 HOURS I WILL:

Father I Thank you for:

-
-
-

I AM A RECOGNIZED THREAT TO DARKNESS BECAUSE:

TRUTH FROM THIS CHAPTER:

NOTES & FREE THOUGHTS:

CHAPTER FOUR

THE WEAPON HELL COULDN'T KILL

BRENDAJEFFERSON.COM

04
CHAPTER FOUR

What if the very wounds that should have written your obituary are instead God's signature that you are the weapon hell could never destroy?

Survival was never the finish line, it was weapons-training. Every plot you outlived, every pit you climbed from, proved that your anointing isn't ornamental; it is yoke-breaking fire that hell cannot snuff out. When you realize obedience, not talent, is your sharpest blade, you step from merely surviving into slaying every chain the enemy forged for you.

The Weapon Hell Couldn't Kill

Some people were born with favor. Others were born with fire.

If you've ever wondered why the enemy couldn't destroy you — despite his best efforts — the answer is simple: you are the weapon he couldn't kill.

You've survived what was meant to bury you. You outlived the plot. You outlasted the pain. And here you are — not just alive, but awakening. And more dangerous than ever before.

The Anointing Is a Weapon

Your anointing isn't a decoration — it's a weapon.

Isaiah 10:27 (KJV) says: "…and the yoke shall be destroyed because of the anointing."

The anointing on your life carries yoke-breaking power. You weren't just anointed to preach, sing, or lead. You were anointed to destroy. And hell knows that. That's why the moment your anointing began to grow, the warfare intensified.

Hell doesn't fight popularity. Hell fights effectiveness.

Survivors Become Slayers

David survived Saul's spears. Joseph survived the pit and the prison. Paul survived shipwrecks, beatings, and betrayal. And you — you've survived depression, rejection, betrayal, failure, and fear.

But survival wasn't the end goal. Survival was your bootcamp.

Because survivors, once healed and whole, become slayers. And slayers shake hell.

When God lets you live through it, He intends to use you as a weapon through it.

The Weapon Is Not What You Think

We often think the weapon is our gifting — but the real weapon is our obedience.

It's our yes when it costs us. It's our peace when we should be panicking. It's our worship when we should be weeping. Hell expected you to die in the process — but you came out prophesying.

That's why Isaiah 54:17 (KJV) says: "No weapon that is formed against thee shall prosper…"

Because God knew the enemy would try. He just wouldn't succeed. Because you were the greater weapon.

God Doesn't Waste Pain

Every tear was training. Every heartbreak was molding. Every betrayal was preparing.

You were being formed — not for pity, but for power.

Romans 8:28 (KJV) reminds us: "And we know that all things work together for good to them that love God, to them who are the called according to his purpose."

You weren't just called. You were crafted.

What the enemy saw as a wound, God saw as a well. And now out of your story flows the oil.

Why You're Still Standing

You're not standing because you're strong — but because God made you resilient. You're not standing because you're lucky — but because you're chosen. You are proof that divine purpose is stronger than demonic plots.

You are walking evidence that God's plan still overrides every attack.

CHAPTER FOUR
FAITH-BUILDING AFFIRMATIONS

01

I survived because God intends to wield me as a living weapon of deliverance

02

The anointing on my life carries yoke-destroying power; no demonic design can stand against it

03

My radical yes to God turns every past pain into present authority and future victory

Reflection: Do You Know What You Carry?

Ask yourself: Do you know what's inside you? Do you know why the enemy's weapons didn't work?

It's because you were one of God's.

Not just saved — sealed. Not just broken — rebuilt. Not just a survivor — a weapon.

Hell aimed at you. But heaven armed you.

You are what hell couldn't kill — and what God is now about to unleash.

Your anointing isn't
a decoration
it's a weapon

THOUGHTS:

_____
_____
_____
_____
_____

5 MINUTE VICTORY JOURNAL

CHAPTER 4
"THE WEAPON HELL COULDN'T KILL"

TAKE A MOMENT TO REFLECT

DATE

S   M   T   W   T   F   S

KEY VERSE FOCUS:

"No weapon that is formed against thee shall prosper…"

— Isaiah 54:17

PRESSURE I FEEL:

_____
_____
_____

IN THE NEXT 24 HOURS I WILL:

_____
_____
_____

Father I Thank you for:

☺ _____
☺ _____
☺ _____

I AM A RECOGNIZED THREAT TO DARKNESS BECAUSE:

TRUTH FROM THIS CHAPTER:

NOTES & FREE THOUGHTS:

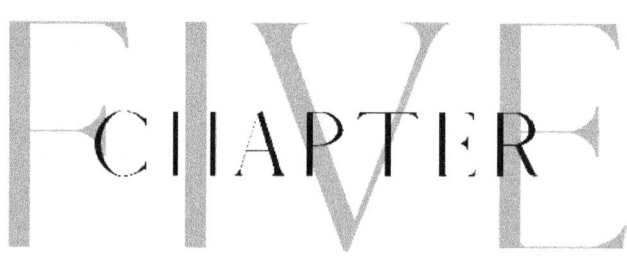

WHEN DESTINY GETS INTERRUPTED

BRENDAJEFFERSON.COM

05
CHAPTER FIVE

When doors slam shut and timelines stall, do you read them as detours or as clues that heaven just protected something priceless inside you?

Hell doesn't interrupt what isn't impending. From Herod's desperate decree to Joseph's pit-stop in prison, the enemy's interference only signals that destiny is on the move and too dangerous to let through unchecked. This chapter flips the script: every delay is heaven's seal over your process, a strategic pause that forges deeper revelation before public release.

INTRODUCTION

When Destiny Gets Interrupted

Every time you pray when you feel empty, demons lose their grip. Every time you worship with tears in your eyes, you announce to darkness, 'I'm still dangerous.' You are a walking zone of purpose. This book is not about feeling sorry for yourself. It's about realizing you're in a war because you are worth fighting for.

It's time to stop asking 'Why me?' and start declaring 'Of course me.' You were built for this fight. You were chosen for this battlefield. You were born for this victory.

If hell sent resistance, heaven sent reinforcement. When hell fights your future, it's because you carry something bigger than you realize. You are carrying seeds, loads, assignments, dreams, a future, influence that hasn't even fully matured yet.

There are moments in your life when everything begins to feel strange — as if you're being pulled back when you're ready to leap forward. Doors close. Delays come. Attacks seem random. But they're not.

Every spiritual interruption is evidence of a heavenly investment.

When God places something weighty in your life — a calling, a destiny, an assignment that will impact others — hell takes notice. And not just notice. It launches interruption campaigns.

The Pattern of Interruption

In Matthew 2, we find a powerful pattern. Jesus was just a child when Herod, influenced by fear and darkness, sent a decree to slaughter innocent boys just to stop one promise.

Why? Because hell sensed what was coming.

Herod wasn't just fighting a baby — he was unknowingly resisting destiny.

When God is about to birth something major, interruptions will come that don't make sense — attacks that feel personal, but are actually strategic.

Interrupted but Not Destroyed

Joseph's journey in Genesis followed a similar line.

He had a dream from heaven — a vision of promotion, favor, and leadership. But immediately after the dream, came interruption:

- His brothers betrayed him.
- He was sold into slavery.
- He was falsely accused.
- He was forgotten in prison.

But not destroyed.

Why? Because divine dreams come with divine preservation.

Hell can interrupt what it cannot cancel.

Heaven's Seal Over Your Process

Sometimes we panic when life doesn't go as planned, but God never panics. He sees the end from the beginning. And what looks like sabotage is often God allowing the shaking that will lead to your sending.

Philippians 1:6 (KJV) declares: "Being confident of this very thing, that he which hath begun a good work in you will perform it until the day of Jesus Christ."

If God started it, hell can't stop it — only stall it. And even delays serve God's purpose.

Interruption Triggers Revelation

When interruptions hit your life, God uses them to reveal three powerful things:

1. Your Strength – You learn that what used to break you now builds you.

2. Your Circle – Not everyone can walk with you into destiny. Interruption exposes loyalty.

3. Your Source – Interruption makes you depend more deeply on God. When everything is shaking, only His voice holds you together.

When Destiny Provokes Warfare

Your calling will provoke conflict.

The moment you align with purpose, expect friction.
The moment you commit to healing, hell assigns distractions.
The moment you prepare to walk in wholeness, familiar spirits from your past try to reappear.

But this is your confirmation. If your life is under attack, it's because heaven has something scheduled through you.

CHAPTER FIVE
FAITH-BUILDING AFFIRMATIONS

01

Every interruption in my journey is proof that heaven has invested greatness in me

02

I may be interrupted, but I will not be destroyed God's seal keeps my destiny intact

03

What tries to delay my purpose today will unveil greater revelation and promotion tomorrow

Reflection: What's Being Interrupted in Your Life?

Think back: What's been delayed? Blocked? Fought against without reason?

Could it be that your warfare isn't about where you are, but about where you're headed?

Don't quit. Don't lose heart.

Every interruption is a sign you are important.

Every resistance is evidence that your presence on this earth is dangerous to darkness.

Heaven's investment in you is too great to let the interruption win.

> Every spiritual interruption is evidence of a heavenly investment

THOUGHTS:

_____
_____
_____
_____
_____
_____

5 MINUTE VICTORY JOURNAL

CHAPTER 5
"WHEN DESTINY GETS INTERRUPTED"

TAKE A MOMENT TO REFLECT

DATE

S   M   T   W   T   F   S

KEY VERSE FOCUS:

"But as for you, ye thought evil against me; but God meant it unto good, to bring to pass, as it is this day, to save much people alive."

—Genesis 50:20

PRESSURE I FEEL:

IN THE NEXT 24 HOURS I WILL:

Father I Thank you for:

I AM A RECOGNIZED THREAT TO DARKNESS BECAUSE:

TRUTH FROM THIS CHAPTER:

NOTES & FREE THOUGHTS:

WHEN HELL RINGS ALARMS

BRENDAJEFFERSON.COM

06

CHAPTER SIX

When pressure spikes the moment you start to wake up to your calling, do you quickly retreat or do you realize the sirens are proof that hell just recognized you?

Hell's alarms don't blare when you fail; they blare when you awaken. The enemy panics the instant you "come to yourself," because an identity-aware believer becomes a movement that dismantles darkness far beyond their own lifetime.

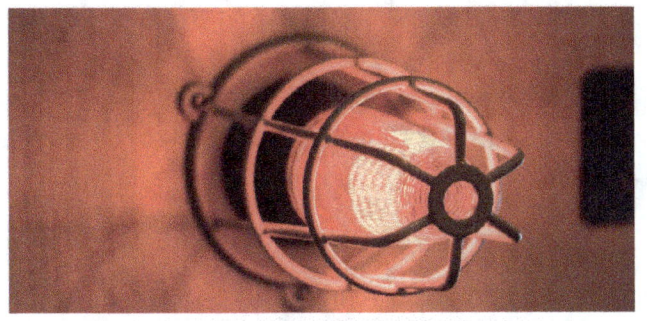

INTRODUCTION

When Hell Rings Alarms

You are carrying answers to problems other people are praying about. You are carrying legacy—the people who will be saved, healed, changed because of your obedience.

Satan is terrified because if you fully walk in what God has placed in you, it will cause ripple effects beyond your lifetime.

Like Paul—he didn't just plant churches in his day; we are still reading his letters 2,000 years later. Paul's life is one massive example of warfare because of destiny.

Before he even fully stepped into his mission, God said something about him in Acts 9:15- 16. Paul was chosen as a vessel. Because of his call, suffering and attacks were part of his journey.

There are moments in the spirit when something shifts — not in the natural first, but in the unseen. It's the moment your name rings out in the realm of hell, not because of failure, but because of awakening.

Hell has alarms.

They sound not when you sin — but when you awaken to who you really are.

When You Wake Up, Hell Gets Nervous

The prodigal son in Luke 15 made many mistakes. But it wasn't until Scripture says, "he came to himself" that everything changed.

That moment was an alarm to hell.

Because when a believer "comes to themselves" — when they shake off shame, rise from regret, and walk back into purpose — all of hell begins to panic.

You are most dangerous when you know who you are.

Heaven Marks You — Hell Tracks You

Before Jesus ever performed a miracle, cast out a demon, or opened a blind eye, He was baptized. And a voice from heaven said:

"This is my beloved Son, in whom I am well pleased." (Matthew 3:17 KJV)

Immediately after, He was led into the wilderness — and Satan showed up.

Why? Because identity triggers warfare.

Before the miracles came the affirmation. Before the assignment was public, hell tried to provoke Him privately.

The Sound of Alignment

When you align your life with God's will — even in silence — hell hears it like thunder.

It sounds like:

- A prayer life that deepens.
- A voice that grows bolder.
- A soul that's healed.
- A heart that says "yes" to purpose.

These moments send ripples through the spirit realm. You may be in your room, but hell is on alert.

Hell Reacts to the Unseen You

Many times, you're not even walking in your full power yet — but the enemy sees it forming.

The conversations you haven't had. The people you haven't reached. The freedom you haven't tasted yet — but it's coming.

So hell responds now. It doesn't wait until you're at the top. It tries to stop you at the bottom.

That's why early attacks are often the fiercest — because you're at the doorway of transformation.

The Alarm Signals Fear, Not Power

When hell attacks, it's not a display of power — it's a display of fear.

You were born to impact things you can't even see yet. You carry influence that hasn't been fully activated. And the enemy knows it.

The alarm doesn't sound for the passive. It sounds for the rising

CHAPTER SIX
FAITH-BUILDING AFFIRMATIONS

01

I am most dangerous when I know who I am hell's alarms prove my awakening

02

Every alarm in hell confirms I am not a mistake but a God-ordained movement

03

My rising identity echoes through darkness, announcing heaven's answers are here

Reflection: Has Your Name Echoed in Hell?

Don't be surprised when things go wrong the moment you start getting right.

Don't shrink back when warfare shows up at the same time as your healing.

It means something is waking up in you.

And hell knows it.

Hell doesn't ring alarms for the defeated — it rings alarms for the dangerous.

And you, child of God, are about to shake kingdoms.

Hell doesn't ring alarms
for the defeated
it rings alarms
for the dangerous

THOUGHTS:

_____
_____
_____
_____
_____
_____

5 MINUTE VICTORY JOURNAL

CHAPTER 6
"WHEN HELL RINGS ALARMS"

TAKE A MOMENT TO REFLECT

DATE

S   M   T   W   T   F   S

KEY VERSE FOCUS:

"And when he came to himself, he said, How many hired servants of my father's have bread enough and to spare, and I perish with hunger!"

—Luke 15:17

PRESSURE I FEEL:

IN THE NEXT 24 HOURS I WILL:

Father I Thank you for:

- ☺
- ☺
- ☺

I AM A RECOGNIZED THREAT TO DARKNESS BECAUSE:

TRUTH FROM THIS CHAPTER:

NOTES & FREE THOUGHTS:

CHAPTER SEVEN

WHEN HELL INVESTIGATES YOUR POTENTIAL

BRENDAJEFFERSON.COM

07
CHAPTER SEVEN

When life suddenly feels like every move is under a microscope, do you see it as harassment or as proof that heaven just flagged your potential and hell launched an inquiry?

Hell never squanders resources on the harmless. The moment your obedience begins to threaten generational strongholds, the enemy files a strategic investigation just as he did with Job and Paul because what you're carrying carries ripple effects hell cannot afford to ignore.

When Hell Investigates Your Potential

Look at the warfare Paul faced. Shipwrecked three times, as mentioned in 2 Corinthians 11:25. Beaten with rods, also in 2 Corinthians 11:25. Stoned and left for dead, recorded in Acts 14:19. Imprisoned multiple times, noted in Acts 16:23-24.

And yet, Paul kept moving—preaching, planting churches, and writing letters that we are still reading today. Why all the attacks? Because hell feared the influence Paul would have on generations.

2 Timothy 4:7 was his final word. Think about it; Paul didn't say 'I avoided a good fight.' He said he fought it and finished it. The enemy fought Paul not to stop him in the moment, but to silence the impact he would have for centuries. The bigger the destiny, the bigger the warfare. Hell fights fiercest against what it fears the most.

You don't just go through storms — you get studied.

When your prayer life deepens, your obedience sharpens, and your "yes" becomes more costly, something begins to happen in the unseen realm: hell launches an inquiry.

Just like heaven recognizes your purpose, hell investigates your potential.

Satan Doesn't Strike Randomly — He Inquires

In Job 1:7-8 (KJV), God asks Satan: "Whence comest thou?"

Satan answers, "From going to and fro in the earth…"

Then God says: "Hast thou considered my servant Job…?"

The word "considered" here means more than a passing glance. In the original Hebrew, it implies a calculated assessment — a strategic investigation.

Hell watches what heaven highlights.

Job's life became a battlefield not because he was weak, but because he was worthy.

You've Been Marked Because You Matter

If your life feels constantly targeted, ask yourself: What does my obedience threaten?

You're not just surviving the enemy — you're frustrating his system. Your very presence in your family line is breaking generational patterns. Your voice is silencing lies. Your story is destroying shame.

You are marked because you matter.

Paul Was Tracked by Hell

In Acts 19:15 (KJV), evil spirits say: "Jesus I know, and Paul I know; but who are ye?"

Hell had Paul on record. Why? Because Paul's life had become a wrecking ball against darkness.

He was healing, preaching, planting, enduring — and heaven was backing him.

When you live with spiritual weight, you gain recognition in both realms.

The Devil Doesn't Waste Resources

Hell doesn't assign warfare to the careless. It doesn't launch full-scale attacks on people who are spiritually asleep. It fights what it fears — and fears what carries fire.

If the enemy is coming for you, it's because he's already seen who you're becoming.

And he knows, once you fully step into it — he can't stop you.

Heaven Brags Before Hell Attacks

Don't miss this: before Job was ever touched, heaven bragged about him.

God said: "There is none like him in the earth, a perfect and an upright man…" (Job 1:8 KJV)

Your battles don't always mean you've done something wrong. Often, they mean you've done something right.

Hell responds to God's endorsement of your life.

CHAPTER SEVEN
FAITH-BUILDING AFFIRMATIONS

01

I am worth investigating my life is evidence that God has entrusted me with kingdom influence

02

Every scrutiny of darkness confirms that heaven has already stamped my destiny with significance

03

I refuse intimidation; what tries to study me today will testify of God's victory through me tomorrow

Reflection: Are You Being Watched?

The reason the pressure has intensified is because the purpose has expanded. You are not just being fought — you are being studied.

But take courage. Every time hell investigates, it confirms heaven's investment.

So walk boldly. Live faithfully. Obey fearlessly.

Because even when hell inquires — heaven still reigns.

Hell watches what heaven highlights

THOUGHTS:

_____
_____
_____
_____
_____
_____

5 MINUTE VICTORY JOURNAL

CHAPTER 7
"WHEN HELL INVESTIGATES YOUR POTENTIAL"

TAKE A MOMENT TO REFLECT

DATE

S   M   T   W   T   F   S

KEY VERSE FOCUS:

"And the LORD said unto Satan, Hast thou considered my servant Job...?"

—Job 1:8

PRESSURE I FEEL:

IN THE NEXT 24 HOURS I WILL:

Father I Thank you for:

-
-
-

I AM A RECOGNIZED THREAT TO DARKNESS BECAUSE:

TRUTH FROM THIS CHAPTER:

NOTES & FREE THOUGHTS:

CHAPTER EIGHT

THE BREAKING THAT BUILT YOU

BRENDAJEFFERSON.COM

08
CHAPTER EIGHT

When life cracks your comfort zone wide open, do you interpret the shatter as defeat or as the sound of God forging something stronger inside you?

Before there is authority, there is almost always agony. Scripture and experience agree: what hell meant to crush you, heaven intends to construct into a platform that carries fresh oil and undeniable power.

INTRODUCTION

The Breaking That Built You

Your current battle is evidence that heaven has already stamped your future with favor.

Now, let's look at Jesus. Hell fought Him before He even spoke a word. Before Jesus even began His ministry, before He healed, preached, or delivered anyone, hell was already trying to kill Him.

Matthew 2:13 recounts how King Herod, influenced by fear and evil, ordered the murder of all male children under two years old, as stated in Matthew 2:16. Why? Because he heard from the wise men that a new king had been born.

Think about it. Jesus was just a child. He hadn't performed one miracle, he hadn't preached one sermon, he hadn't raised one dead body. And yet, hell stirred up kings and murderers to try and kill Him early.

Everyone wants the oil — but no one wants the crushing.

Everyone wants the power — but few want the process.

But the truth is: before there is authority, there is almost always agony.

What hell tried to break in you, God used to build you.

You Are a Product of Crushing, Not Convenience

In Luke 22:44 (KJV), Jesus is in Gethsemane, and Scripture says: "Being in an agony he prayed more earnestly: and his sweat was as it were great drops of blood falling down to the ground."

Gethsemane means "oil press." Jesus wasn't just praying — He was being crushed.

But out of that crushing came the strength to endure the cross.

Out of the breaking came the victory of resurrection.

You don't walk in power until you've wept in private.

Your Pain Was Preparing Your Platform

We often try to hide our pain — but pain is often the very thing God uses to make us usable.

Moses was broken in the wilderness before he ever stood before Pharaoh.

David was rejected by his family before he ever reigned as king.

Esther had to hide her identity before she could reveal her purpose.

Your story isn't proof of defeat — it's proof of development.

Why Didn't It Kill You?

Because it was never meant to. It was meant to form you.

Jeremiah 18:4 (KJV) says: "And the vessel that he made of clay was marred in the hand of the potter: so he made it again another vessel, as seemed good to the potter to make it."

Even when your life was broken, you were still in His hands.

That mistake? Still in His hands. That betrayal? Still in His hands. That failure? Still in His hands.

You weren't discarded — you were re-shaped.

Your Authority Comes From What You Survived

The enemy doesn't mind your testimony if it's shallow. But when you've bled and battled, when you've cried and kept going, your testimony becomes a threat.

That's why Revelation 12:11 (KJV) declares: "And they overcame him by the blood of the Lamb, and by the word of their testimony…"

The blood covered you. Your story confirms it.

The Breaking Is Part of the Becoming

You can't carry healing without knowing what it feels like to hurt.

You can't release freedom until you've walked through your own chains.

What felt like a breaking season was actually a birthing season.

And what you carry now will crush what used to control you.

CHAPTER EIGHT
FAITH-BUILDING AFFIRMATIONS

01

I am a product of crushing, not convenience my breaking is birthing unstoppable strength

02

My pain was preparing my platform: the authority I carr rises from what I survived

03

What hell tried to break in me, God is now using to build others, releasing fresh oil through my story

Reflection: What Did the Breaking Birth in You?

Think about it. You almost quit — but you didn't. You almost died in it — but you rose.

You're not here by accident. You're here because you were chosen to carry the kind of oil that only comes from the crush.

That pain didn't ruin you. It revealed you.

You are more than what happened to you. You are what God built from it.

What hell tried to break in you, God used to build you

THOUGHTS:

_____
_____
_____
_____
_____

5 MINUTE VICTORY JOURNAL

CHAPTER 8
"THE BREAKING THAT BUILT YOU"

TAKE A MOMENT TO REFLECT

DATE

S M T W T F S

KEY VERSE FOCUS:

"For our light affliction, which is but for a moment, worketh for us a far more exceeding and eternal weight of glory."

—2 Corinthians 4:17

PRESSURE I FEEL:

IN THE NEXT 24 HOURS I WILL:

Father I Thank you for:

I AM A RECOGNIZED THREAT TO DARKNESS BECAUSE:

TRUTH FROM THIS CHAPTER:

NOTES & FREE THOUGHTS:

THE PURPOSE BEHIND THE PRESSURE

BRENDAJEFFERSON.COM

09
CHAPTER NINE

When every forward step attracts fresh resistance, do you view it as a signal to retreat or as evidence that heaven just confirmed your next level?

Pressure is rarely random. In Scripture and in your story, the enemy only erects roadblocks where destiny is about to break ground; resistance is heaven's spotlight revealing that your obedience is already shaking darkness.

INTRODUCTION

The Purpose Behind the Pressure

Why? Because Satan knew, if Jesus grew up, if Jesus walked into His assignment, if Jesus fulfilled His destiny, hell's authority would be shattered forever.

John 10:10—The enemy tried to steal Jesus' life early because he feared what Jesus would accomplish later.

Later in Jesus' ministry, more attacks came. Satan tempted Jesus fiercely after 40 days of fasting, as recorded in Matthew 4. Religious leaders constantly tried to trap Him, accuse Him, and stone Him.

Why so much warfare? Because the greater the purpose, the greater the pressure.

Hell feared the impact of Jesus fully walking out His mission. And when Jesus fulfilled it, when Jesus declared on the cross, 'It is finished' as stated in John 19:30, He marked the ultimate victory over all the powers of darkness, forever changing the course of history.

There's a kind of resistance that doesn't make sense on the surface.

Every door you knock on seems sealed. Every step you take feels like a pushback. The question rises: What am I doing wrong?

But what if you're doing everything right?

Sometimes, resistance isn't punishment — it's revelation. It's not a sign to turn back, but a sign that you're heading in the right direction.

The Enemy Doesn't Resist What Isn't a Threat

In 1 Thessalonians 2:18 (KJV), Paul says: "Wherefore we would have come unto you… but Satan hindered us."

The word "hindered" means to cut off, obstruct, or block. Paul wasn't in sin. He was in purpose. Yet, the enemy resisted him — because of the impact his obedience would produce.

When your "yes" carries weight, it will provoke warfare.

You're Not Just Being Fought — You're Being Identified

Resistance becomes personal when your destiny becomes dangerous.

If you ever wonder why everything got harder the moment you got serious about God… it's because the resistance is proof of identity.

You are not who you used to be. You've been marked.

And hell knows that if you keep moving forward, something will break open.

God Uses Resistance to Refine You

Resistance is not just from the enemy. Sometimes, God allows it to:

• Sharpen your discernment • Expose your dependencies • Reveal your source of strength

James 1:3-4 (KJV) says: "The trying of your faith worketh patience. But let patience have her perfect work, that ye may be perfect and entire, wanting nothing."

Resistance matures what convenience can't.

Every Pushback Has a Purpose

Joseph was resisted by his brothers. Moses was resisted by Pharaoh. Nehemiah was resisted by Sanballat and Tobiah. Jesus was resisted by religious leaders and Satan himself.

In every case, the resistance confirmed the mission.

The warfare was an echo of their assignment.

You're not under attack just because you're weak — you're under attack because you're necessary.

CHAPTER NINE
FAITH-BUILDING AFFIRMATIONS

01

I am not merely opposed: I am being identified as a threat to hell's agenda

02

Every pushback is purposeful God is refining my character to match my calling

03

The greater the pressure, the greater the purpose God is birthing through me

Reflection: What Has Resistance Been Revealing in You?

Has resistance exposed where your faith truly stands? Has it brought hidden fears to the surface? Has it forced you to depend on God more deeply?

Then it has done its job.

You are being refined. Strengthened. Equipped.

Resistance is not a stop sign — it's a signal: You're getting closer.

Don't stop. Don't settle.

Push through — because on the other side of resistance is revelation… and release.

The greater the purpose, the greater the pressure

THOUGHTS:

_____
_____
_____
_____
_____
_____

5 MINUTE VICTORY JOURNAL

TAKE A MOMENT TO REFLECT

DATE

S M T W T F S

CHAPTER 9
"THE PURPOSE BEHIND THE PRESSURE"

KEY VERSE FOCUS:

"My brethren, count it all joy when ye fall into divers temptations; knowing this, that the trying of your faith worketh patience."

—James 1:2-3

PRESSURE I FEEL:

IN THE NEXT 24 HOURS I WILL:

Father I Thank you for:

☺ _____
☺ _____
☺ _____

I AM A RECOGNIZED THREAT TO DARKNESS BECAUSE:

TRUTH FROM THIS CHAPTER:

NOTES & FREE THOUGHTS:

CHAPTER TEN

THE WEAPON HELL COULDN'T KILL — YOU

BRENDAJEFFERSON.COM

10

CHAPTER TEN

When you replay every hit you've survived, do you call it luck or do you recognize it as proof that you were God's secret weapon all along?

The enemy never intended for you to make it this far. Yet every blow that should have buried you only forged "war-tested strength," announcing to darkness that the very weapon it formed could not prosper because you are the weapon God preserved for this hour.

The Weapon Hell Couldn't Kill — You

He didn't just save mankind, He stripped hell of its authority, as stated in Colossians 2:15.

Hell fought Paul because his life would echo for generations. Hell fought Jesus early because it feared the destiny He carried. Hell fought Job because he was marked for a double blessing, and hell fights you because you are carrying something powerful that will impact more than you can currently see.

Let's look at Job. Notice something shocking: Job wasn't attacked because he was bad; he was attacked because he was righteous and blessed. In Job 1:8, God Himself brags on Job's faithfulness. Satan immediately accuses Job, implying that Job only serves God because he's blessed. Job 1:7, 10—Here, Satan challenges the integrity of Job's devotion, suggesting that his faithfulness is merely due to the blessings he has received.

This accusation sets the stage for the trials that Job would face, demonstrating not just the resilience of his faith but also the depth of his character in the face of unfathomable challenges.

There's a reason you're still here.

You've faced things that could have shattered you — but you survived.

You've carried wounds no one sees — and yet you worship.

You've been betrayed, forgotten, lied on, abandoned — and still, you haven't let go of God.

That's not weakness. That's war-tested strength.

You are the weapon hell tried to destroy... but couldn't.

You Weren't Supposed to Survive

Let's be honest — if the enemy had his way, you would've been swallowed up by depression, addiction, anger, bitterness, guilt, or shame.

But Isaiah 54:17 (KJV) declared over you: "No weapon that is formed against thee shall prosper..."

It didn't say weapons wouldn't be formed. It said they wouldn't win.

You were hit — but not held. Wounded — but not wasted. Fallen — but not forsaken.

Why? Because you were God's secret weapon.

Your Survival Was Strategic

The enemy saw your potential before you did. That's why the attacks came early. That's why they were so fierce. Because you carry something dangerous to darkness.

- Your story silences shame.
- Your survival gives others permission to hope.
- Your wounds have become weapons of intercession.

You're not just a survivor — you're a solution.

Jesus Was the Weapon Hell Never Understood

1 Corinthians 2:8 (KJV) says: "Which none of the princes of this world knew: for had they known it, they would not have crucified the Lord of glory."

Hell thought the cross was the end. But it was actually the entry point to victory.

The same is true for you. What was supposed to take you out… took you in — deeper into calling, anointing, and divine alignment.

The Weapon Has a Voice

Psalm 107:2 (KJV) says: "Let the redeemed of the Lord say so…"

Why does the weapon still speak? Because the weapon that couldn't be killed becomes a witness.

Every scar, every testimony, every breakthrough is a sound of war in the enemy's camp.

You may not feel loud — but in the spirit, you're thunder.

CHAPTER TEN
FAITH-BUILDING AFFIRMATIONS

01

I am the weapon hell could not kill—my survival is strategic, not accidental

02

No weapon formed against my destiny can win; every scar now speaks of Christ's victory through me

03

What threatened to crush me has commissioned me to carry power that dismantles darkness

Reflection: What Hasn't Killed You Has Commissioned You

If you're still standing, you're still called. If you're still breathing, you're still chosen. You were never just a target — you were a threat. Hell had a plan. But God had a purpose. And that purpose is rising.

Because the weapon hell couldn't kill... was you.

You are the weapon hell tried to destroy... but couldn't

THOUGHTS:

_____

_____

_____

_____

_____

_____

5 MINUTE VICTORY JOURNAL

CHAPTER 10
"THE WEAPON HELL COULDN'T KILL—YOU"

TAKE A MOMENT TO REFLECT

DATE

S M T W T F S

KEY VERSE FOCUS:

"I shall not die, but live, and declare the works of the LORD."

—Psalm 118:17

PRESSURE I FEEL:

IN THE NEXT 24 HOURS I WILL:

Father I thank you for:

☺ _____
☺ _____
☺ _____

I AM A RECOGNIZED THREAT TO DARKNESS BECAUSE:

TRUTH FROM THIS CHAPTER:

NOTES & FREE THOUGHTS:

CHAPTER ELEVEN

FAITH IN THE FIRE

BRENDAJEFFERSON.COM

11
CHAPTER ELEVEN

When the heat rises and everything familiar melts away, do you view the flames as a funeral pyre—or as Heaven's forge shaping an indestructible you?

From Job's double-portion restoration to three Hebrew boys walking unbound in a furnace, Scripture shouts that fire is not permitted to finish God's people—only to fashion them. The blaze you're in is proof of value, not vulnerability; some fires don't consume, they confirm who you really are and reveal the Fourth Man standing with you.

Faith in the Fire

Satan couldn't touch Job without permission because God had a hedge around him. Job's favor, character, and relationship with God provoked hell.

Job was attacked because he was dangerous to hell's agenda. Hell feared what Job represented—a man who would not curse God even when everything was stripped.

Remember, Job endured the attack. His faith remained intact. In the end, God restored double for everything he lost, as recorded in Job 42:10.

Hell fought Job because God had marked him for double blessings, not because he was weak.

How hell fights you. Satan uses a strategic, repeated pattern to try to abort or derail your destiny. This pattern reflects a targeted approach designed to challenge those who carry a significant potential to impact the kingdom of God.

Some come out of the fire scorched and silent.

But some come out of the fire with something sacred — the flame of glory, the sound of survival, the oil of endurance.

When you've been through the fire and still believe, you don't just carry scars — you carry power.

The Fire Was Not to Burn You — But to Build You

In Daniel 3, Shadrach, Meshach, and Abednego were thrown into a literal furnace for refusing to bow to the king's idol.

But Daniel 3:25 (KJV) says: "Lo, I see four men loose, walking in the midst of the fire, and they have no hurt; and the form of the fourth is like the Son of God."

God didn't keep them from the fire — He joined them in it.

And they came out:

- Without burns
- Without bondage
- But with boldness

Because some fires don't consume — they confirm.

Refined, Not Reduced

Malachi 3:3 (KJV) says: "And he shall sit as a refiner and purifier of silver..."

A refiner never takes their eyes off the silver. They watch it until they can see their reflection in it. That's what your fire did. It didn't reduce you — it refined you. God used it to burn away fear, insecurity, doubt, and pride — until you looked like Him.

Your Flame Is Not from Men — It's from Encounter

There is a difference between a fire given by man and a flame lit by God. Jeremiah 20:9 (KJV) says: "His word was in mine heart as a burning fire shut up in my bones..."

When you've survived what should have killed you, you carry something hell can't counterfeit: unshakeable fire. This is the fire that fuels your calling, purifies your motives, and ignites others.

CHAPTER ELEVEN
FAITH-BUILDING AFFIRMATIONS

You're Dangerous Because You're Flame-Proven

Satan fears people who've been through flames and didn't come out faithless. People who say:

- "I still trust Him."
- "I still worship."
- "I still believe."

Hell hoped the fire would silence you — but instead, you became a torch.

01

I emerge from every furnace refined, not reduced carrying boldness hell cannot silence

02

My scars are signatures of survival: they testify that God uses heat to hard-forge hope

03

The flame upon my life is Heaven-lit, unshakeable, and contagious igniting freedom in others

Reflection: What Has the Fire Left You With?

If the fire didn't consume you, ask yourself: what did it create in you?

- Did it ignite a new level of dependence on God?
- Did it purify your motives?
- Did it reveal your calling?

You're not just a survivor of fire. You are a carrier of flame.

And that flame is setting other captives free.

The fire was not to burn you but to build you

THOUGHTS:

_____
_____
_____
_____
_____
_____

5 MINUTE VICTORY JOURNAL

CHAPTER 11
"FAITH IN THE FIRE"

TAKE A MOMENT TO REFLECT

DATE

S   M   T   W   T   F   S

KEY VERSE FOCUS:

"Lo, I see four men loose, walking in the midst of the fire, and they have no hurt; and the form of the fourth is like the Son of God."

—Daniel 3:25

PRESSURE I FEEL:

IN THE NEXT 24 HOURS I WILL:

Father I Thank you for:

I AM A RECOGNIZED THREAT TO DARKNESS BECAUSE:

TRUTH FROM THIS CHAPTER:

NOTES & FREE THOUGHTS:

CHAPTER TWELVE

THE ALARM OF YOUR ASSIGNMENT

BRENDAJEFFERSON.COM

12
CHAPTER TWELVE

Why does the warfare spike the moment you decide to obey could it be that your simple "yes" triggers alarms in hell?

Hell never sounds sirens over the indifferent; it panics when a believer rises with purpose. Every prayer you whisper and every act of obedience you choose dents darkness proof that heaven has anointed what hell has feared from the start.

INTRODUCTION

The Alarm of Your Assignment

Fear and intimidation make you feel too small, too unworthy, too late, too broken.

As stated in 2 Timothy 1:7, fear paralyzes you before you even take the first step.

Discouragement and weariness tire you out emotionally, mentally, spiritually, so you start questioning the call, as noted in Galatians 6:9.

Discouragement is a slow attack; it makes you stop watering the seed you carry.

Distractions and detours pull your attention off your real assignment—relationships, offenses, unnecessary battles, shining but empty opportunities, as illustrated in Luke 10:40- 42.

Satan doesn't have to destroy you if he can distract you.

Attacks on your identity make you forget who you are in Christ, as highlighted in Matthew. If you doubt who you are, you'll doubt what you're carrying.

You may not see it, but every time you get back up, every time you pray when you're weary, worship while wounded, or speak truth when you're trembling — hell is alarmed.

Hell doesn't tremble because you're perfect. Hell trembles because you're persistent.

Why Hell Pays Attention to You

Psalm 149:6-7 (KJV) says: "Let the high praises of God be in their mouth, and a twoedged sword in their hand; To execute vengeance upon the heathen, and punishments upon the people."

- When you open your mouth in praise — you sound like war.
- When you walk in purpose — you shake regions.
- When you declare truth — you disrupt strongholds.

That's why hell sets off alarms when you rise each morning with a "yes" still in your spirit.

You're not just living. You're resisting.

Every Move You Make Is a Threat

- Every prayer you pray dents the darkness.
- Every act of obedience weakens the enemy's grip.
- Every soul you encourage adds pressure to hell's gate.

You're not a weak wanderer. You're a walking weapon.

Hell knows that if you ever fully believe who you are, if you ever step fully into your identity, if you ever refuse to bow — you'll become a spiritual explosion.

The Sound of the Alarm

In Acts 19:15 (KJV), the evil spirit said: "Jesus I know, and Paul I know; but who are ye?"

You know what that means? Hell keeps records. There are names that echo in darkness. Your resistance has made you known. The question isn't whether hell is watching.

The question is — what is it seeing?

Heaven Has Anointed What Hell Has Feared

Every alarm in hell is proof: You're not a mistake. You're a movement. You may not feel like it. You may not always see it. But your life is interrupting the enemy's plans. That's why the attacks have been relentless.

That's why the pressure has been high.

It's because you're not just carrying breakthrough — you are one.

CHAPTER TWELVE
FAITH-BUILDING AFFIRMATIONS

01

My persistent obedience makes hell tremble fear has no veto over my assignment

02

Every step I take in purpose is a strike against the kingdom of darkness

03

I am not a passive wanderer; I am a walking weapon forged by God

Reflection: What Sound Does Your Life Make in the Spirit?

When you wake up, does hell go silent? Does it tighten its grip? Does it panic?

You weren't made to blend in. You were born to set off alarms in the kingdom of darkness. Every prayer. Every praise. Every time you choose faith over fear.

You are sounding an alarm — and hell has no answer for your endurance.

> **You're not
> a weak wanderer
> you're a walking weapon**

THOUGHTS:

_____
_____
_____
_____
_____
_____

5 MINUTE VICTORY JOURNAL

CHAPTER 12
"THE ALARM OF YOUR ASSIGNMENT"

TAKE A MOMENT TO REFLECT

DATE

S   M   T   W   T   F   S

KEY VERSE FOCUS:

"Submit yourselves therefore to God. Resist the devil, and he will flee from you."

—James 4:7

PRESSURE I FEEL:

IN THE NEXT 24 HOURS I WILL:

Father I thank you for:

- ☺
- ☺
- ☺

I AM A RECOGNIZED THREAT TO DARKNESS BECAUSE:

TRUTH FROM THIS CHAPTER:

NOTES & FREE THOUGHTS:

CHAPTER THIRTEEN

VICTORY IN THE VALLEY

BRENDAJEFFERSON.COM

13
CHAPTER THIRTEEN

When the landscape of your life sinks into a shadowed valley, do you assume you've been demoted or do you discern that God just enrolled you in advanced training?

The valley is never a permanent address; it is Heaven's outdoor classroom, where endurance is forged and God's voice echoes the clearest. What feels like confinement is actually refinement, proving you are already equipped to walk through and walk out with a testimony hell can't silence.

Victory in the Valley

What happens when we give in? The seed, the dream, calling, destiny remains buried. Delay and discouragement set in. Future generations miss what we were supposed to release.

But remember, God's grace can redeem time, as Joel 2:25 says, 'I will restore to you the years.'

What should we look out for? Spiritual exhaustion after taking steps of obedience, unexplainable battles right when you are about to birth something new. Sudden attacks on your self-worth, identity, or God's promises. Increased distractions and unnecessary drama.

These are not random. They are signs you're nearing something major.

How should we be encouraged? James 1:2-4 tells us, 'Trials are proof of promotion. Hell fights hardest when you're wearing breakthrough.' God is using even the warfare to sharpen, mature, and anoint you more deeply.

There are places in your journey where it feels like everything is in the valley — your hopes, your dreams, even your spirit. The mountaintop is a distant memory, and all that remains is the weight of the present.

But it is here, in the valley, where the most powerful transformations happen.

The Valley Is Not Your Home, But It's Your Training Ground

Psalm 23:4 (KJV) says: "Yea, though I walk through the valley of the shadow of death, I will fear no evil: for thou art with me; thy rod and thy staff they comfort me."

It's significant that David didn't say, "I live in the valley," but "I walk through the valley."

The valley is temporary. It's not where you're meant to stay.

But in it, you find God in a way you couldn't on the mountaintop.

The Valley Reveals What's Inside of You

The valley is where pressure hits, and pressure reveals what you're really made of. It's in the moments when you feel like giving up that you realize how much strength God has deposited inside of you.

The apostle Paul spoke of suffering as a way of pressing us into spiritual maturity:

Romans 5:3-4 (KJV): "And not only so, but we glory in tribulations also: knowing that tribulation worketh patience; And patience, experience; and experience, hope."

The valley is where your character is sharpened. The valley is where you become stronger, sharper, and more aware of God's presence than ever before.

The Valley Is Where You Hear His Voice Clearly

Sometimes the silence in the valley is the loudest voice you'll hear.

When everything else seems uncertain, when distractions are gone, you can hear the gentle whisper of God leading you.

Isaiah 30:21 (KJV): "And thine ears shall hear a word behind thee, saying, This is the way, walk ye in it, when ye turn to the right hand, and when ye turn to the left."

It's in the valley where you can't rely on your own strength, and that's when you begin to hear God most clearly.

You Are Equipped to Survive the Valley

God doesn't lead you into valleys that you can't survive. When He says, "Walk through," He is assuring you that you have what it takes to make it out stronger than before.

2 Corinthians 4:8-9 (KJV): "We are troubled on every side, yet not distressed; we are perplexed, but not in despair; Persecuted, but not forsaken; cast down, but not destroyed."

You are equipped to survive and thrive in the valley because the One who is with you is greater than the obstacles you face.

Victory Is in the Valley

The valley doesn't end in defeat — it ends in victory.

Hosea 2:15 (KJV): "And I will give her vineyards from thence, and the valley of Achor for a door of hope…"

The valley of Achor, the valley of trouble, is where God promises a door of hope.

It is in these low places that God will transform your pain into purpose.

CHAPTER THIRTEEN
FAITH-BUILDING AFFIRMATIONS

01 The valley is not my home; it is my training ground for greater victories

02 Pressure in the valley reveals the strength God has already deposited inside me

03 I am fully equipped to survive and triumph in every valley season

Reflection: What Have You Learned in Your Valleys?

• What have the valleys you've walked through revealed about your character and your faith?
• How has God's presence shaped your experience in the low places? • What victory can you claim today because of what you've survived?

The valley is not your final destination. It's where God builds you up, molds you, and prepares you for the next season.

You may walk through the valley, but you won't stay there.

> **The valley is not your home, but it's your training ground**

THOUGHTS:

_____
_____
_____
_____
_____
_____

5 MINUTE VICTORY JOURNAL

CHAPTER 13
"VICTORY IN THE VALLEY"

TAKE A MOMENT TO REFLECT

DATE

S   M   T   W   T   F   S

KEY VERSE FOCUS:

"Yea, though I walk through the valley of the shadow of death, I will fear no evil: for Thou art with me; Thy rod and Thy staff they comfort me."

—Psalm 23:4

PRESSURE I FEEL:

_____
_____
_____

IN THE NEXT 24 HOURS I WILL:

_____
_____
_____

Father I Thank you for:

☺ _____
☺ _____
☺ _____

I AM A RECOGNIZED THREAT TO DARKNESS BECAUSE:

TRUTH FROM THIS CHAPTER:

NOTES & FREE THOUGHTS:

CHAPTER FOURTEEN

WHEN GOD SAYS LIVE

BRENDAJEFFERSON.COM

14
CHAPTER FOURTEEN

When your vision looks sealed in a grave, do you pronounce the story finished or dare you ask what happens when God whispers, "Live"?

The Author of life specializes in resurrection: He speaks to dry bones, long-buried dreams, and forgotten callings, and they stand up again. In this chapter we learn that His command to live is not a momentary miracle but an invitation to partner with Him prophesying, obeying, and watching dead things breathe once more.

When God Says Live

You are carrying answers. You are carrying solutions. You are carrying freedom for someone else.

Hell fights because heaven has already written the ending, and it's a victorious one, as Isaiah 54:10 confirms.

The enemy fights what he cannot stop, only delay. But if you endure, you will hear my battle cry—'My designation is: I am chosen, I am equipped, I am a threat to hell and a weapon in God's hand. I will not back down. I will finish my race, I will birth my destiny, and I will impact generations. No weapon formed against me shall prosper. I win because Jesus already won.'

In the darkest moments of life, when everything seems lost, when your dreams feel like they've been buried, God has a way of resurrecting the dead things — things you thought could never come back. He speaks life into dry bones, and what was once lifeless becomes a living testimony of His power.

God's Power to Bring Dead Things Back to Life

Ezekiel 37:1-5 (KJV) says: "The hand of the Lord was upon me, and carried me out in the spirit of the Lord, and set me down in the midst of the valley which was full of bones, And caused me to pass by them round about: and, behold, there were very many in the open valley; and, lo, they were very dry. And he said unto me, Son of man, can these bones live? And I answered, O Lord God, thou knowest. Again he said unto me, Prophesy upon these bones, and say unto them, O ye dry bones, hear the word of the Lord."

God speaks life into the dead things — and His word carries the power to make them live again.

God Calls the Dead Things by Name

When God speaks life into something, He doesn't speak to the general circumstance. He speaks to the specific dead thing.

He doesn't just say, "I will bring life to you." He says, "Live!" to the bones, to the dreams, to the vision, to the promises that seem long buried.

Isaiah 43:19 (KJV): "Behold, I will do a new thing; now it shall spring forth; shall ye not know it? I will even make a way in the wilderness, and rivers in the desert."

When God speaks over your life, it's a declaration of new life and restoration. He knows where to breathe His life into you, where your purpose needs resurrection.

The Power of Your Prophesy

In Ezekiel 37, God told Ezekiel to prophesy over the dry bones. That's the same calling He has placed on your life.

When you speak His word over your situation, over your dreams, over your calling, you are partnering with His divine power to bring life.

Romans 4:17 (KJV): "As it is written, I have made thee a father of many nations, before him whom he believed, even God, who quickeneth the dead, and calleth those things which be not as though they were."

This is the same power that raised Jesus from the dead — the power to call things that are not as though they were — and He has given it to you.

Resurrection Is Not Just a One-Time Event

Jesus didn't just resurrect to show His power over death. He resurrected to show you that there is no dead thing that God cannot bring to life.

When He calls you to live, He's calling your purpose to live. He's calling your calling to live. He's calling the destiny He has planned for you to come back to life.

John 11:43-44 (KJV): "And when he thus had spoken, he cried with a loud voice, Lazarus, come forth. And he that was dead came forth, bound hand and foot with graveclothes: and his face was bound about with a napkin. Jesus saith unto them, Loose him, and let him go."

When God calls your purpose to life, there will be a process of loosening — a process of freedom from the things that once bound you.

Resurrection Comes Through Obedience

When God speaks life into dead things, He invites you to participate in the resurrection. It's through obedience to His voice that you experience His transformative power.

The miracle of resurrection isn't just about God calling you alive; it's about you responding to His call.

You don't remain where you were. You rise.

CHAPTER FOURTEEN
FAITH-BUILDING AFFIRMATIONS

01

The Word of the Lord breathes life into every dry place of my destiny nothing is beyond resurrection

02

My prophetic voice joins Heaven to call dead dreams by name and command them to rise

03

Obedience positions me for resurrection; I refuse the grave and choose to live

Reflection: What Dead Things Is God Calling to Life in You?

• What dreams have you buried because you thought they were impossible?

• What parts of your life have felt abandoned, like they could never come back to life?

• How is God calling you to prophesy life into your situation?

Remember, no matter how dead your circumstances feel, no matter how much you've lost, God has the final say.

And He says: Live.

> **No matter how dead your circumstances feel, God has the final say and He says: Live**

THOUGHTS:

_____
_____
_____
_____
_____
_____

5 MINUTE VICTORY JOURNAL

CHAPTER 14
"WHEN GOD SAYS LIVE"

TAKE A MOMENT TO REFLECT

DATE

S M T W T F S

PRESSURE I FEEL:

IN THE NEXT 24 HOURS I WILL:

KEY VERSE FOCUS:

"Thus saith the Lord GOD unto these bones; Behold, I will cause breath to enter into you, and ye shall live."

—Ezekiel 37:5

Father I thank you for:

I AM A RECOGNIZED THREAT TO DARKNESS BECAUSE:

TRUTH FROM THIS CHAPTER:

NOTES & FREE THOUGHTS:

CHAPTER FIFTEEN

DECLARATIONS & THE AFTERMATH OF WAR

BRENDAJEFFERSON.COM

15

CHAPTER FIFTEEN

After the smoke of battle clears, do you label the wreckage as the end of your story or dare you declare, "This is my new beginning"?

God never lets the last strike of the enemy be the last word over your life. The "aftermath" is His construction zone, where declarations turn ruins into runways and wounds into wisdom, launching you into a future stronger than the fight that preceded it.

Declarations & The Aftermath of War Declarations:

1. Declare: No weapon that is formed against thee shall prosper.

Isaiah 54:17 - No weapon that is formed against thee shall prosper; and every tongue that shall rise against thee in judgment thou shalt condemn. This is the heritage of the servants of the LORD, and their righteousness is of me, saith the LORD.

2. Declare: I have power, love, and a sound mind, not fear

2 Timothy 1:7 - For God hath not given us the spirit of fear; but of power, and of love, and of a sound mind.

3. Declare: The good work in me will be finished.

Philippians 1:6 - Being confident of this very thing, that he which hath begun a good work in you will perform it until the day of Jesus Christ:

4. Declare: My due season is coming; I refuse to faint.

Galatians 6:9 - And let us not be weary in well doing: for in due season we shall reap, if we faint not.

5. **Declare**: I am more than a conqueror.

Romans 8:37 - Nay, in all these things we are more than conquerors through him that loved us.

6. **Declare**: I have authority over all the enemy's power.

Luke 10:19 - Behold, I give unto you power to tread on serpents and scorpions, and over all the power of the enemy: and nothing shall by any means hurt you.

7. **Declare**: God is my strength; I will not fear.

Psalm 27:1 - The LORD is my light and my salvation; whom shall I fear? the LORD is the strength of my life; of whom shall I be afraid?

The Aftermath Isn't Your Final Chapter — It's Your New Beginning

When a battle ends, the effects linger, but God doesn't allow the aftermath to define you. Instead, He uses it to prepare you for the next level.

In 2 Samuel 11:1-2, we see that after the battle, David was at rest in his palace, but the enemy knew where he was vulnerable.

It's easy to rest and think the war is done, but the enemy is relentless, trying to find an opportunity to attack. However, this doesn't mean we should live in fear — it means we need to be vigilant and resilient.

The aftermath is God's opportunity to build you up stronger than before.

From Wounds to Wisdom

Your wounds are not just scars of survival — they're testimonies of transformation.

They are markers of battles you've fought and won, battles that left you scarred, but scarred with wisdom, strength, and grace.

2 Corinthians 12:9 (KJV): "And he said unto me, My grace is sufficient for thee: for my strength is made perfect in weakness…"

Your wounds are not signs of weakness. They are signs that God's strength has been made perfect in you.

The Rebuilding Process — Strength in the Ruins

In Nehemiah 2:17 (KJV), Nehemiah tells the people: "Ye see the distress that we are in… come, and let us build up the wall of Jerusalem…"

Just because the battle is over, it doesn't mean the rebuilding is easy. After the storm, the ruins can be overwhelming.

But God doesn't leave you in the rubble. He gives you the strength to rebuild from the ground up.

• You rebuild with purpose. • You rebuild with faith. • You rebuild with the wisdom gained through your battles.

Resilient Faith — What Keeps You Standing

There are moments when all you want to do is give up. But it's in these moments that your resilient faith steps in.

Romans 8:37 (KJV): "Nay, in all these things we are more than conquerors through him that loved us."

Even after the battle, you are still more than a conqueror. Your victory is sealed through Christ.

Reflecting on What You've Survived

You may look at the aftermath and think, How can I move forward from this?

But it's essential to see this time of rebuilding as part of your growth.

Every brick you lay, every moment of healing, every step you take in faith is preparation for the next phase of your journey.

God doesn't waste the aftermath. He uses it to prepare you for even greater victories ahead.

CHAPTER FIFTEEN
FAITH-BUILDING AFFIRMATIONS

1. I decree that the aftermath is not my final chapter it is Heaven's blueprint for a brand-new beginning

Every scar is proof of survival and a gateway to greater wisdom: God's strength is perfected in my former wounds

I rise from the ruins with resilient faith, rebuilding in the same place where darkness once tried to bury me

Reflection: How Will You Move Forward from the Aftermath?

- What parts of your life feel like ruins that need rebuilding?

- How has God's grace been sufficient to bring you through the battle?

- What will you do now to rebuild with resilience and faith?

The battle may have taken its toll, but you are still standing, and with God's strength, you will rebuild and restore.

The aftermath isn't your final chapter it's your new beginning

THOUGHTS:

_____

_____

_____

_____

_____

_____

5 MINUTE VICTORY JOURNAL

TAKE A MOMENT TO REFLECT

DATE

S M T W T F S

CHAPTER 15
"DECLARATIONS & THE AFTERMATH OF WAR"

KEY VERSE FOCUS:

"Behold, I will do a new thing; now it shall spring forth..."

— Isaiah 43:19

PRESSURE I FEEL:

IN THE NEXT 24 HOURS I WILL:

Father I thank you for:

I AM A RECOGNIZED THREAT TO DARKNESS BECAUSE:

TRUTH FROM THIS CHAPTER:

NOTES & FREE THOUGHTS:

CHAPTER SIXTEEN

HOW TO USE SCRIPTURE BULLETS

BRENDAJEFFERSON.COM

16
CHAPTER SIXTEEN

What would change if every verse you recited felt less like a lullaby and more like a loaded round that empties hell's chambers?

God never intended His Word to be politely admired; He designed it to be deployed. This chapter shows you how to chamber the promises of Scripture speaking them aloud, weaving them into prayer, memorizing them for instant use, posting them where your eyes land first, declaring them over your identity each day, and remembering that an unseen army backs every bullet you fire .

How to Use Scripture Bullets

In every spiritual battle, the enemy is not afraid of your emotions — he's afraid of your sword. The Word of God is not just encouragement; it is your weapon. It doesn't just inspire — it invades. The enemy knows that when a believer starts speaking the Word with faith and authority, his territory begins to crumble.

Ephesians 6:17 (KJV) "And take the helmet of salvation, and the sword of the Spirit, which is the word of God."

You have been given divine ammunition. These are not just verses — they are bullets of breakthrough, arrows of authority, and declarations of dominion. But the power is not just in having them. The power is in how you use them.

1. Speak Them Out Loud

The devil is not omniscient — but he hears what you say. When you declare the Word out loud, you shift the atmosphere around you and reinforce your spirit within you. Why it matters: Jesus didn't fight Satan in the wilderness with silence. He fought with "It is written." (See Matthew 4:4) Activation Tip: Each morning, declare at least one scripture aloud with boldness. Let your house hear it. Let hell hear it.

2. Incorporate Into Prayer

Don't just talk to God — agree with God. Mix His Word into your prayers. The Word is His will, and when you speak it, Heaven responds. John 15:7 (KJV) "If ye abide in me, and my words abide in you, ye shall ask what ye will, and it shall be done unto you." Activation Tip: Pray the Word. Example: "Lord, You said no weapon formed against me shall prosper (Isaiah 54:17), and I declare that today."

3. Memorize for Instant Use

When the enemy attacks suddenly, you won't have time to scroll for scripture. You need it hidden in your heart, ready to fire. Psalm 119:11 (KJV) "Thy word have I hid in mine heart, that I might not sin against thee." Activation Tip: Choose one scripture a week to memorize and meditate on. Speak it daily until it becomes part of you.

4. Visible Reminders

Seeing the Word activates the Word. Place scriptures on your mirrors, doors, and dashboards. Let your eyes feed your faith.

Deuteronomy 6:6-9 (KJV) "And thou shalt write them upon the posts of thy house, and on thy gates." Activation Tip: Create "Word Zones" in your home — places where the Word is always visible and vocal.

5. Daily Declaration of Identity

The greatest battle is over your identity. When you remind yourself of who you are, you silence the lies of the enemy. Say aloud daily: "I belong to Jesus. I am hidden in Him. His blood covers me. His Spirit fills me. His Word arms me." Activation Tip: Write this declaration somewhere permanent. This is your spiritual battle cry.

CHAPTER SIXTEEN
FAITH-BUILDING AFFIRMATIONS

01

When I speak God's Word out loud, I fire spiritual rounds that hell cannot dodge

02

Every verse I memorize becomes an instant-access weapon, ready the moment resistance appears

03

Resistance only proves recognition—if hell is resisting me, Heaven is reinforcing me

6. Remember Divine Support

Resistance is proof of recognition. If hell is resisting you, it's because Heaven is reinforcing you. 2 Kings 6:16 (KJV) "Fear not: for they that be with us are more than they that be with them." Truth: You are not fighting alone. You are backed by Heaven's army. You are not hell's victim — you are its fear.

> **You are not hell's victim
> you are its fear**

THOUGHTS:

_____
_____
_____
_____
_____
_____

5 MINUTE VICTORY JOURNAL

CHAPTER 16
"HOW TO USE SCRIPTURE BULLETS"

TAKE A MOMENT TO REFLECT

DATE

S M T W T F S

KEY VERSE FOCUS:

"And take the sword of the Spirit, which is the word of God."

—**Ephesians 6:17**

PRESSURE I FEEL:

IN THE NEXT 24 HOURS I WILL:

Father I Thank you for:

- ☺
- ☺
- ☺

I AM A RECOGNIZED THREAT TO DARKNESS BECAUSE:

TRUTH FROM THIS CHAPTER:

NOTES & FREE THOUGHTS:

CHAPTER SEVENTEEN

THE PROOF THAT HELL FAILED

BRENDAJEFFERSON.COM

17
CHAPTER SEVENTEEN

When you trace the scars on your story, do you see them as disfigurements or as living receipts that hell's best shot wasn't enough?

This chapter is a victory audit. Every mark you carry every survived attack, every fire you outlasted is courtroom evidence that heaven's seal on your life could not be broken. Your very breath rebukes the accuser and announces, "Hell failed."

The Proof That Hell Failed

Spiritual Warfare Declaration

In the name of Jesus, I rebuke every spirit of fear, discouragement, and distraction. I bind you and cast you out of my mind, my heart, and my path. I loose focus, boldness, and divine acceleration into my life right now.

This is not just spiritual talk. This is spiritual warfare. Every word you speak in faith is a missile launched into the enemy's camp.

Hell Fought You Because Heaven Built You

The intensity of your warfare is a clue to the weight of your calling. You weren't just made to survive — you were built to shake systems and awaken generations. The same God who created you also equipped you with everything you need to win.

Your Scars Will Preach

Victory is beautiful, but scars are powerful. Scars tell the story of what tried to kill you and failed. They are visible reminders that grace carried you through the fire.

John 20:27 (KJV): "Then saith he to Thomas, Reach hither thy finger, and behold my hands... be not faithless, but believing."

Even Jesus used His scars to reveal truth. Your scars will speak louder than your titles, degrees, or platforms.

Qualified by the Fire

The fire didn't come to destroy you — it came to distinguish you.

1 Peter 1:7 (KJV): "That the trial of your faith, being much more precious than of gold that perisheth, though it be tried with fire..."

God allowed the fire to reveal what hell couldn't see — your endurance, your resilience, your fight.

Hell Should Have Finished You — But God Sealed You

You were sealed by God's Spirit before the enemy ever launched his attack.

Ephesians 1:13 (KJV): "...after that ye believed, ye were sealed with that holy Spirit of promise."

You were stamped with purpose. Chosen with intention. Protected with firepower from Heaven.

You Are Living Proof

Every breath you take is proof that the devil failed. Every morning you rise is evidence that God's plan is still active.

Revelation 12:11 (KJV): "And they overcame him by the blood of the Lamb, and by the word of their testimony…"

You are not here by accident — you are here on assignment. And your life is the loudest sermon hell will ever hear.

CHAPTER SEVENTEEN
FAITH-BUILDING AFFIRMATIONS

01 I am living proof that the devil's plan failed each inhale testifies of God's triumph

02 I was sealed by God's Spirit before the battle began: no assault can erase Heaven's stamp on my destiny

03 My scars preach louder than any platform, proclaiming that grace carried me through the fire and qualified me for greater purpose

Reflection: What Is Your Survival Saying?

- What battle did you make it through that should have ended you?
- What does your survival say about God's promises?
- How can you turn your scars into testimonies that set others free?

Your survival is not just for you. It's for every person watching you, following you, and hoping they too can rise.

Let your life be the evidence that the enemy's best wasn't enough.

Every breath you take
is proof that
the devil failed

THOUGHTS:

----

5 MINUTE VICTORY JOURNAL

CHAPTER 17
"THE PROOF THAT HELL FAILED"

TAKE A MOMENT TO REFLECT

DATE

S   M   T   W   T   F   S

KEY VERSE FOCUS:

"And they overcame him by the blood of the Lamb, and by the word of their testimony."

—**Revelation 12:11**

PRESSURE I FEEL:

IN THE NEXT 24 HOURS I WILL:

Father I Thank you for:

- ☺
- ☺
- ☺

I AM A RECOGNIZED THREAT TO DARKNESS BECAUSE:

TRUTH FROM THIS CHAPTER:

NOTES & FREE THOUGHTS:

CHAPTER EIGHTEEN

PRAYER AND DECLARATION OF IDENTITY

18
CHAPTER EIGHTEEN

When you lift your voice in prayer, do you simply hope God is listening or do you realize you're legislating identity in the spirit realm?

Prayer is more than conversation; it is combat loaded with kingdom authority. Every declaration you speak out of God's Word becomes spiritual legislation that shifts the battlefield, re-centers your identity, and announces to darkness that you are praying from victory, not for it.

INTRODUCTION

Prayer and Declaration of Identity

Before you can walk in power, you must pray with authority. This prayer is more than words—it's warfare. Every line is a weapon. Every declaration is an act of spiritual resistance. As you speak this aloud, know that heaven backs your voice and hell recognizes your authority. You are not praying from weakness—you are praying from victory.

Prayer and Declaration

Father, in the Name of Jesus,

I thank You that You have called me, appointed me, and anointed me for such a time as this.
You have planted Your purpose inside of me,
And no weapon formed against me shall prosper.

I declare that I am not small,
I am not powerless, I am not abandoned.
I am a carrier of destiny,
I am an answer to someone's cry.
I am light in darkness.

I am bold as a lion because the righteous are bold.
I have not been given a spirit of fear, but of power, love, and a sound mind.

Every spirit of discouragement, distraction, and doubt,
I break your assignment in the Name of Jesus.

In You, O Lord, do I put my trust and confidently take refuge;
Let me never be put to shame or confusion! (Psalm 7:1)

Living From the Place of Declaration

Declarations are not suggestions; they are spiritual legislation. When you speak truth, you shift the battlefield. This prayer re-centers your identity, aligns your posture, and silences every lie from the enemy.

Your words matter. Proverbs 18:21 says, 'Death and life are in the power of the tongue...' Use your voice to shape your reality.

Scriptural Foundation

- Esther 4:14 - You were born for such a time as this.
- Isaiah 54:17 - No weapon formed against you shall prosper.
- 2 Timothy 1:7 - God has not given you a spirit of fear.
- Proverbs 28:1 - The righteous are bold as a lion.
- Psalm 7:1 - In God we take refuge and shall never be put to shame.

CHAPTER EIGHTEEN
FAITH-BUILDING AFFIRMATIONS

01 Heaven backs my voice my prayers are weapons, and hell recognizes my authority

02 Declarations are not suggestions; they establish the atmosphere of my life and break every lie of the enemy

03 I speak life, courage, and destiny over myself; no weapon formed against me shall prosper

Reflection: What Are You Speaking Over Yourself?

- Are your words empowering your identity or feeding your fears?
- What lies have you unknowingly agreed with that must be broken?
- How can you reinforce your daily walk with declarations rooted in Scripture?

Speak life. Speak faith. Speak boldly.

Declarations are not suggestions; they are spiritual legislation

THOUGHTS:

_____
_____
_____
_____
_____
_____

5 MINUTE VICTORY JOURNAL

CHAPTER 18
"PRAYER AND DECLARATION OF IDENTITY"

TAKE A MOMENT TO REFLECT

DATE

S M T W T F S

KEY VERSE FOCUS:

> "Death and life are in the power of the tongue: and they that love it shall eat the fruit thereof."
>
> —Proverbs 18:21

PRESSURE I FEEL:

IN THE NEXT 24 HOURS I WILL:

Father I Thank you for:

☺ _____
☺ _____
☺ _____

I AM A RECOGNIZED THREAT TO DARKNESS BECAUSE:

TRUTH FROM THIS CHAPTER:

NOTES & FREE THOUGHTS:

CHAPTER NINETEEN

A DECLARATION OF ENDURANCE

BRENDAJEFFERSON.COM

19
CHAPTER NINETEEN

When fatigue roars louder than your vision, will you quit or will you recognize the moment as God's cue to draw on supernatural stamina?

Weariness is real, but so is the power of Christ coursing through you. Heaven never asked you to sprint forever only to finish so every wave of exhaustion becomes the proving ground where divine strength takes over and hell's hope of stopping you collapses

A Declaration of Endurance

Weariness is real. But so is your power in Christ. The moments where your strength feels gone are the exact moments where divine strength begins to take over. You're not commanded to run every day at full speed—you're commanded to finish. This is not just a prayer; it's a declaration of spiritual stamina.

Declaration of Endurance

I command weariness to lift off me now.

I bind every lie spoken against my future and I loose the truth of God over my life. I am chosen. I am equipped. I am unstoppable through Christ who strengthens me. Lord, open my eyes to see beyond the warfare into the victory You already prepared.

Strengthen my hands for battle and my heart for endurance. Teach me to recognize the enemy's strategies early and to rise above them with wisdom and patience. I declare over myself:

I will not give up.
I will not throw away my confidence.
I will not bury my gift.
I will finish my race.

When Endurance Is the Weapon

Endurance doesn't just get you through — it crushes the enemy's hope that you'll quit. The enemy doesn't fear your start; he fears your finish. When you choose to endure, you declare that your faith is not circumstantial — it's anchored in Christ.

Scriptural Foundation

• Hebrews 10:35-36 (KJV) - "Cast not away therefore your confidence, which hath great recompence of reward."

• Galatians 6:9 (KJV) - "And let us not be weary in well doing: for in due season we shall reap, if we faint not."

• 2 Timothy 4:7 (KJV) - "I have fought a good fight, I have finished my course, I have kept the faith."

• Philippians 4:13 (KJV) - "I can do all things through Christ which strengtheneth me."

CHAPTER NINETEEN
FAITH-BUILDING AFFIRMATIONS

01

I refuse to quit endurance is my weapon, crushing the enemy's hope that I'll walk away

02

I am chosen, equipped, and unstoppable through Christ who infuses me with strength

03

I will finish my race; every step forward silences the lies spoken against my future

Reflection: Are You Still Running?

- What area of your life feels hardest to endure right now?
- What lies have tried to convince you to quit or bury your gift?
- How is God calling you to finish strong despite the pressure?

Endurance is a declaration that God is not finished with you yet. Keep going.

> **66**
>
> Endurance doesn't just
> get you through
> it crushes the enemy's hope
> that you'll quit

THOUGHTS:

_____

_____

_____

_____

_____

_____

5 MINUTE VICTORY JOURNAL

CHAPTER 19
"A DECLARATION OF ENDURANCE"

TAKE A MOMENT TO REFLECT

DATE

S M T W T F S

KEY VERSE FOCUS:

"And let us not be weary in well doing: for in due season we shall reap, if we faint not."

—Galatians 6:9

PRESSURE I FEEL:

IN THE NEXT 24 HOURS I WILL:

Father I thank you for:

☺
☺
☺

I AM A RECOGNIZED THREAT TO DARKNESS BECAUSE:

TRUTH FROM THIS CHAPTER:

NOTES & FREE THOUGHTS:

CHAPTER TWENTY

CHARGE: HEAVEN'S WEAPON, HELL'S THREAT

BRENDAJEFFERSON.COM

20
CHAPTER TWENTY

After walking through nineteen chapters of spiritual bootcamp, will you retreat or will you charge forward as the weapon heaven forged and hell fears?

This closing charge reminds you that survival was only stage one; now you rise to build, birth, and break chains. Everything you've endured has tempered you into an atmosphere-shifter and generation-changer hell's opposition is simply the scoreboard proving you're already dangerous.

INTRODUCTION

Charge: Heaven's Weapon, Hell's Threat

You haven't just been reading words - you've been undergoing a spiritual bootcamp. Every page has reminded you that your life has weight, your voice has power, and your calling is costly. Hell fights what it fears, and if you've been through fire, pressure, betrayal, and warfare - then you, child of God, are one of Heaven's most dangerous weapons.

This is your reminder: You are an atmosphere-shifter, a generation-changer, a bloodline-redeemer. You are not here to merely survive - you are here to build, to birth, to break chains, and to leave a legacy of faith.

Declaration

I will birth what You placed inside me.
I will impact more than I can see.
The seeds I am sowing now will harvest in generations to come.
I cover my mind, my heart, my purpose, and my steps under the blood of Jesus.
I decide I will not die in the fight. I will live to testify.

In Jesus' mighty name, Amen.

Charge Forward

Everything you've survived has brought you to this moment. Not to collapse. Not to quit. But to rise. You are rising from ashes with authority. You are emerging from pain with purpose. You are walking out of fear with fire.

Your story is moving forward - because what God placed in you is not just for you; it's for the world. Hell has tried to stop you because it saw who you would become if you ever healed, if you ever stepped into wholeness, if you ever fully believed what God has already spoken over your life.

This is your charge: Keep praying. Keep believing. Keep pushing. The oil on your life cost you something - and now it's time to pour it out.

Scriptural Charge to Keep Moving

- Philippians 1:6 (KJV) - "He which hath begun a good work in you will perform it until the day of Jesus Christ."

- 2 Timothy 4:7 (KJV) - "I have fought a good fight, I have finished my course, I have kept the faith." - Psalm 118:17 (KJV) - "I shall not die, but live, and declare the works of the Lord."

CHAPTER TWENTY
FAITH-BUILDING AFFIRMATIONS

01

I am heaven's weapon and hell's threat; the battles I survived certify my authority

02

The work God began in me will be perfected I will fight the good fight. finish my course. and keep the faith

03

I will not die but live to declare the works of the Lord; my testimony will ignite freedom for generations

Reflection: You Are the Weapon

- What have you survived that proves you're still a threat to the enemy?
- What are you carrying that must now be released?
- Who are you called to impact beyond this page?
- How will you walk differently now, knowing what you carry?

You are not just reading this message - you are being called to live it out. Step forward boldly. Lift your head high. Sharpen your sword. Hell fights what it fears. And it fears you.

Hell fights what it fears
And it fears you!

THOUGHTS:

_____

_____

_____

_____

_____

_____

5 MINUTE VICTORY JOURNAL

TAKE A MOMENT TO REFLECT

DATE

S M T W T F S

CHAPTER 20
"CHARGE: HEAVEN'S WEAPON, HELL'S THREAT"

KEY VERSE FOCUS:

"Thou art My battle-axe and weapons of war: for with thee will I break in pieces the nations, and with thee will I destroy kingdoms."

—Jeremiah 51:20

PRESSURE I FEEL:

IN THE NEXT 24 HOURS I WILL:

Father I Thank you for:

-
-
-

I AM A RECOGNIZED THREAT TO DARKNESS BECAUSE:

TRUTH FROM THIS CHAPTER:

NOTES & FREE THOUGHTS:

CHAPTER TWENTY ONE

MY PERSONAL TESTIMONY

BRENDAJEFFERSON.COM

21
CHAPTER TWENTY-ONE

When a loved one seems buried beneath consequences, can you still believe God is writing resurrection into their story?

In this closing testimony, Dr. Brenda pulls back the curtain on her son Pastor Jimmy's ten-year incarceration a season that could have ended in tragedy but instead birthed a global movement of hope. Her journey proves that when a mother refuses to surrender her praise, prison walls become pulpits and prodigals come home transformed.

MY PERSONAL TESTIMONY

As I come to the close of this book, I cannot end without sharing one of the deepest, most personal journeys of my life - the story of my son, Pastor Jimmy.

Yes, my son made mistakes. He did things that were not right, things that led him to be incarcerated for ten years. As a mother, watching your child go through something like that is a pain no words

can fully describe. But through it all, I never gave up on him. I never stopped praying. I never stopped believing that God could reach him, even behind prison walls.

Out of this painful season, I wrote the song "Never Give Up." I poured my heart into the message that no matter how dark it seems, no matter how long the wait, you have to keep praising God while you wait. That truth became the foundation of my book You've Got to Praise Him While You Wait and sparked the Mothers of Incarcerated movement - a passion to encourage mothers everywhere who are interceding for their children, whether they are in prison physically, emotionally, or spiritually.

What I learned in those years is that hell fights what it fears. The enemy fought hard to take my son. The enemy fought hard to destroy his purpose, his future, his voice. But God prevailed. Even though

Pastor Jimmy went through prison, God used that very place as the soil to raise him up as a voice of hope. In prison, he led others to Christ. He ministered, he preached, and he became a light in a dark place. And when God brought him home, he didn't come home the same - he came home transformed.

Today, Pastor Jimmy is a living testimony, a champion for those who are struggling, a voice for redemption, restoration, and renewal. His life is a constant reminder that no matter how far someone goes, no matter how broken their path, God's love reaches deeper. God's power redeems fully.

To every mother reading this - I know the tears you've cried. I know the nights you've stayed awake, interceding, pleading, believing for your child. And I am here to tell you: don't stop. Don't give up. Keep standing. Keep praying. Keep praising.

Hell fights what it fears. And if the enemy is fighting your child, it's because they are marked with purpose. You are not just a mother - you are a warrior. Your prayers are shaking heaven and shaking hell.

As I close this book, I declare over you and your family: You will see the goodness of the Lord. You will see restoration. You will see your child rise, just as I have seen mine. And together, we will continue to be living witnesses that no weapon formed against us shall prosper.

Final Prayer and Blessing

My prayer is that as you have read this book - chapter by chapter, line by line - something has been stirred deep within you.

From Chapter 1 all the way through Chapter 21, you have been taken on a journey through spiritual warfare, purpose, identity, resilience, breakthrough, and destiny.

My prayer is that this book has not only spoken to your mind, but has ministered to your spirit. That every testimony, every scripture, every declaration has reminded you that:

- You are not weak - you are a weapon.
- You are not forgotten - you are favored.
- You are not under attack because you are failing - you are under attack because you are feared by the enemy.

As you turn the final page, I pray that you feel commissioned to walk out what you've learned.

That you rise in faith.

That you carry every truth, every promise, every spiritual weapon you've gained - and go forward boldly into the destiny God has placed on your life.

This book is not the end. It's the launching point.

So go forth, knowing that hell fights what it fears - and heaven fights for what it loves. And you, child of God, are both feared by hell and fiercely loved by heaven.

With all my love and prayers,

Dr. Brenda

CHAPTER TWENTY-ONE
FAITH-BUILDING AFFIRMATIONS

01 My persistent prayers shake both heaven and hell no prison, physical or spiritual, can silence God's purpose over my family

02 Hell fights what it fears: opposition over my child is evidence of their divine assignment

03 I stand as a warrior-parent: I will never give up, never stop praising, and I will see restoration with my own eyes

> Hell fights what it fears.
> And if the enemy
> is fighting your child,
> it's because they are
> marked with purpose

THOUGHTS:

_____
_____
_____
_____
_____
_____

5 MINUTE VICTORY JOURNAL

CHAPTER 21
"MY PERSONAL TESTIMONY"

TAKE A MOMENT TO REFLECT

DATE

S M T W T F S

KEY VERSE FOCUS:

"For this my son was dead, and is alive again; he was lost, and is found."

—Luke 15:24

PRESSURE I FEEL:

_____
_____
_____

IN THE NEXT 24 HOURS I WILL:

_____
_____
_____

Father I Thank you for

☺ _____
☺ _____
☺ _____

I AM A RECOGNIZED THREAT TO DARKNESS BECAUSE:

TRUTH FROM THIS CHAPTER:

NOTES & FREE THOUGHTS:

CONCLUSION

THE SOUND OF YOUR RISING

BRENDAJEFFERSON.COM

THE SOUND OF YOUR RISING
Hell heard the tremor before you felt it

Every page you have just walked through every verse underlined, every journal line scratched in faith has cracked the silence that once covered your destiny. The enemy's alarms are proof, not of your weakness, but of your arrival. You are no longer the one wondering why the fight found you; you are the one who has discovered who you are in the fight. You have learned that weapons are not forged in comfort. They are hammered in hardship, cooled in tears, and lifted by hands that refuse to let go. You survived the furnace so you could carry the fire; you endured the valley so you could speak life to others still in shadows. Every interruption became an invitation. Every breaking became a birthing. Every scar became a signature that reads, "Property of Heaven Unauthorized use by hell denied."

Now, hear Heaven's commissioning echo over your story:

"Arise, shine; for thy light is come, and the glory of the LORD is risen upon thee."
—Isaiah 60:1 KJV

THE COMMISSION

The Commission
1. Arise.
2. Stand in the full stature of your calling. Let the posture of your spirit declare that you are done shrinking to fit other people's fears.
3. Shine.
4. Brilliance is not pride; it is obedience. Illuminate the corridors of your workplace, your family, your generation with the undeniable glow of a life set on holy fire.
5. Advance.
6. Move forward with Scripture on your tongue and compassion in your hands. Pray for the sick. Speak hope to the hopeless. Break cycles in your bloodline. Build what God shows you in midnight visions.
7. Announce.
8. Tell your testimony without editing out the pain. Hell's greatest embarrassment is the sound of its own failure reverberating through your redeemed voice.

A FINAL DECLARATION

Take a deep breath. Read this slowly out loud and sign your amen:
"I am heaven's weapon and hell's greatest fear.
 I rise from the ashes of every battle fearless and free.
 I carry the fire of God, the wisdom of scars,
 and the unstoppable love of Jesus Christ.
 I will fight the good fight, finish my course, keep the faith,
 and leave a trail of freedom behind me.
Hell fought me because it feared me and it lost.
 Amen."

A CLOSING PRAYER

Father, for the reader whose hands now close this book, I ask for a fresh baptism of courage. Let dormant dreams resurrect, strangled callings breathe, and timid prayers roar. Drench every chapter they have read with present-tense power let the truths leap from ink to incarnation. May angels be assigned to guard, guide, and gather the harvest their obedience will reap.

Where chains once rattled, let worship rise. Where night once lingered, let dawn break. Where fear once shouted, let Your still small voice thunder hope. In the undefeated name of Jesus,
 Amen.

YOUR NEXT STEP

Do not shelve these pages as a finished story live them as a daily strategy. Return to the 5-Minute Victory Journal whenever the battle intensifies. Quote the declarations until they feel like the drumbeat of your heart. And when you meet another weary warrior, hand them your copy scribbles, tear-stains, and all because weapons multiply when they are shared.

Lift your head. Square your shoulders. Hell knows your name and Heaven has already written "victorious" beside it.

Now, go shake nations.

BRENDA JEFFERSON
Author

Dr Brenda Jefferson is essential to the body of Christ. Her passion for the Word of God, gospel music, worship, and her creative ability to write, allows her to inspire others in a positive way. She is a bright light in the lives of many, embarking for change and calling others toward Holiness.

Through the mission and ministry of her husband, Bishop M.B. Jefferson, she is Co-Pastor of Living in Victory Christian Church, Deeper Life Christian Church, and World Assemblies Fellowship International. She also helps to oversee The House of David Help Center and is CEO of Scripture Music Group. With ministry at the forefront of her heart, she is submissive to the call of God on her life. Together, they work diligently to release strongholds, unite relationships, deliver those bound from addiction, empower the youth, and be a united influence for Jesus. In these uncertain times of pandemic, poverty, wars, and famine, she is necessary for this generation. Her 'last days' message of repentance, faith, and good works captivates the masses. Through truth and humility, she is devoted to her assignment and seeks to help those in need.

NOTES:

NOTES:

NOTES:

NOTES:

BRENDAJEFFERSON.COM

NOTES:

BRENDAJEFFERSON.COM

www.ingramcontent.com/pod-product-compliance
Lightning Source LLC
Chambersburg PA
CBHW071238070526
44583CB00017B/2234